To my friend, Howard Lamar ---
May yer trails be free of grizzlies!

Eating Up the Santa Fe Trail

Hope you find this book fun!

Waugh!

Sam'l P. Arnold

Eating Up the Santa Fe Trail

Sam'l P. Arnold

& Illustrated by Carrie Arnold

UNIVERSITY PRESS OF COLORADO

Published by the University Press of Colorado
P. O. Box 849, Niwot, Colorado 80544

First Edition

The University Press of Colorado is a cooperative publishing enterprise supported, in part, by Adams State College, Colorado State University, Fort Lewis College, Mesa State College, Metropolitan State College, University of Colorado, University of Northern Colorado, University of Southern Colorado, and Western State College.

The paper used in this publication meets the minimum requirements of the American National Standard for Information Sciences—Permanence of Paper for Printed Library Materials. ANSI Z39.48–1984

Library of Congress Cataloging-in-Publication Data

Arnold, Sam, 1926–
      Eating up the Santa Fe Trail / Sam'l P. Arnold; & illustrated by Carrie Arnold. — 1st ed.
          p.   cm.
      Includes bibliographical references and index.
      ISBN 0-87081-186-x (alk. paper). — ISBN 0-87081-187-8 (pbk.: alk. paper)
      1. Cookery, American—Western style. 2. Santa Fe Trail—History. 3. West (U.S.) History—1848–1950. 4. West (U.S.)—Social life and customs. I. Title.
TX15.2.W47A76 1990
641.5978—dc20   90-48412
                                                              CIP

This book is dedicated to those western historians, both professional and amateur, who love to climb on board the time machine, each in their own way, and return to the Old West for "fat buffler and shinin' times."

The Mountain Man Toast

HERE'S TO THE CHILDS WHATS COME AFORE,
AND HERE'S TO THE PILGRIMS WHATS COME ARTER,
MAY YER TRAILS BE FREE OF GRIZ,
YER PACKS FILLED WITH PLEWS,
AND FAT BUFFLER IN YER POT!
WAUGH!

— Sam and Carrie Arnold
Peter and Mary Olch

Contents

Preface   xi

Acknowledgments   xv

Chapter 1: Wagons Ho!   1

Beginnings of the Santa Fe Trail; William Becknell; Franklin; Arrow Rock; Henry Nave's pigs; **Rhubarb Stalks Pie, or Persian Apple;** Arrow Rock dinner; Boone's Lick; Lexington; Fort Osage; Independence; Westport; emigrant staples; gourmet goods; The Catfish House at Westport's Harris House Hotel; **To Fry Catfish;** Wagon Train Messes; Mahaffie House; **Shaker Chicken Fricassee;** Hays House in Council Grove; **Roasting Beef;** Oysters; Salt Pork and Bacon; **Recipe for Salt Pork; Pois de Trappeur;** "His Bread . . . It Was Corn Dodgers"; Noah Smithwick; **Green Corn Fritters; New England Corn Cake; St. Charles Hotel Corn Bread; Virginia Corn Bread; Boston Corn Bread; Indian Loaf Cake; Johnnie Cake; Spider Corn Cake; Southern Cornmeal Pone, or Corn Dodgers;** San Jacinto Corn; Hominy, or Nixtamal; Sourdough; **Recipe for Sourdough Starter and Bread;** biscuits; *entre dos fuegos;* healthfulness of sourdough bread; "Billy Seldom" and "Johnny Constant"; Fried Bread, or Doughnuts; **Olykoeks (Oily Cakes, or Raised Doughnuts).**

Chapter 2: Thirst on the Trail   21

Cups of Java, or How to Make Coffee; Arbuckle Bros.; **Camp Fire Coffee;** Tea, Herbal Teas, and Hot Chocolate; chokecherry, pipsissewa, and other herbal teas; **Recipe for Hot Chocolate;** Whiskey, Belly Washes, and Aguardientes; Monongahela and Allegheny whiskey; bourbon; "Quentoque y Tenaysi juisque" (Kentucky and Tennessee whiskey); temperance movement; Fort Union (of the north); liquor trade with the Indians; E. C. Booz and fancy bottles; "Great Father's Milk"; **Injun Whiskey;** "hailstorm"; aguardiente; glass bottles' value; Cocktails; bitters;

Peychaud; **Sazerac;** Jerry Thomas's **Martinez Gin Cocktail;**
Hot Brandy and Rum Punch; Real Georgia Mint Julep;
Rum; descriptions of various rums; **Tom & Jerry; Rocky**
Mountain Punch; Applejack; Shrubs; **Raspberry Shrub;**
Rum Shrub.

Chapter 3: Meeting the Buffalo on the Prairie   33
    Lewis Garrard's wagon train in the summer of 1846;
warm liver; raw marrow; **Buffalo en Appolas;** Mexican Buffalo Hunters (ciboleros); Buffalo Jerky, or Carne Seca; Preparing Carne Seca, or Jerky; Marrow Bones; Boudins;
Buffalo Tongue (served at the Maxwell House and
Delmonico's); **Cooking a Buffalo Tongue; Moose Nose;**
Tolling Antelope; Skunk; Wild Birds and Fish by the Arkansas.

Chapter 4: Contact with the Indians   43
    Indian Enemies; Diluted or Doped Alcohol; Fort Lara-
mie doped alcohol; Indian Trading; trading practices in Indian villages; Colonel Dodge and Mexican liquor in 1835;
Dog Stew; Garrard's first dog stew; Cheyenne dishes; Pemmican; Indian Delicacies; Paunch Cooking; Wo-ja-pi; **Rec-**
ipe for Wo-ja-pi; Was-nah; Wash-tunk-ala; Prairie
Potatoes and Commote; Fry Bread; **Squaw Bread;** acorn
biscuits; Piñon Nuts (in soup); Innards; gall as a dyspepsia
cure; Chokecherry Tea; pincherry and sumac teas;
Kinnikinnik; Indian Cooking Tools; Indian Dining Protocol; A Repulsive Meal; dried buffalo lung, buffalo blood
jelly, and moose nose.

Chapter 5: Military Forts on the Trail   59
    Need for military protection of trains and settlers; Fort
Marcy, Fort Union, Fort Osage, Fort Leavenworth; joys and
miseries of military mess; cooking in camp and on bivouac;
salt pork on a stick; letter from Fort Larned; Fort Larned
store selling lobster; **Hardcrackers, or Hard Tack; Army**
Bread; sutler's stores; caviar; Bent, St. Vrain & Company;
Apple Pie Without Apples, or Mock Apple Pie; Fort Riley,
Fort Zarah, Fort Larned, Fort Dodge, Fort Mann (Atkinson); rum ration dispensed until 1850, when replaced by
coffee; Kearney's army; Mexican War sardine cans; **Salt**
Pork with Mashed Peas; Plain Irish Stew; Suet Dump-
lings; Turkish Pilaf; Broiled Mackerel; Stewed Oysters;

Indian Meal Pudding; Spruce Beer; **Recipe for Spruce Beer;** Mormon Battalion dishes; **St. Jacob's Soup; Finker; Colcannon.**

Chapter 6: The Fur Traders and Bent's Fort   71

Cimarron cutoff and mountain route to Santa Fe; culinary life at Bent, St. Vrain & Company's adobe fort; work staff; visitors; Barclay's comments; inventory lists; Bent's Water Biscuits; Charlotte Green; **Pumpkin Pie; Slap Jacks; Pickled Devil's Claws;** Good Times and Fandango; an evening's entertainment; Wine at Bent's Fort; valuable glass bottles; balsam bitters and pepper sauce; Chinese ginger; taffy pulls; **Molasses Taffy;** Bent's attitude toward liquor trade; **Hailstorm; Wassail;** Beaver Tail.

Chapter 7: From Bent's Fort
and on Into New Mexico   83

Bent's Fort; cooling drinks and refrescos; **Horchata; Four-Seed Horchata;** Colonche and Lemonade with Chia; Atole and Chaquehue; **Almond Atole;** Pinole; **Champurrado; Mexican Pot Coffee;** Taos Lightning; **Taos Hanging Eggnog;** Spanish primer eggnog; **Old-Time Eggnog;** Corn-Sugar Molasses; Kearney's army entry into New Mexico; Las Vegas, San Miguel del Vado, Pecos; giant snake legend; New Mexican grapes; Wine Production in El Paso.

Chapter 8: Spaniard, Mexican, and Indian   93

Rancho de las Golandrinas; Indian pueblos of Rio Grande; **Machaca de Huevo; Sopa de Vermicelli;** Mistela; **Recipe for Mistela; Chimajá Whiskey; Licor de Yerba Buena; Biscochitos; Sopaipillas Made with Yeast; Sopaipillas Made with Baking Powder;** Honey; **Stewed Hen in Red Chile;** Susan Magoffin Discovers New Mexican Delights; **Sopa de Arroz; Pollo Relleno; Corn and Bean Soup;** Garbanazos; **Garbanzos with Chile;** Hot Chocolate; **Mexican Chocolate; Mexican Chocolate, Short Version;** chocolate history; The Market; bread; Santa Fe Newspaper Ads; New Mexican Cuisine; Corn Tortillas; Piki; Tamales; **Recipe for Tamales;** Hominy Corn (Posole); **Posole (Hog and Hominy); Posole with Pork and Green Chile; Trotter Posole;** Chiles; **Basic Red Chile Puree; Village-Style Chile con Carne; Carne Adobada;** Dicho (a Saying); The Best

Chile?; medicinal uses for chile; chiles in witchcraft; Desserts; **Arroz Dulce;** Cajeta; **Cajeta de Leche; Eagle Brand Cajeta; New Mexico Goat's Milk Cheese; Requesones;** Capirotada; **Recipe for Capirotada; Budin de Garbanzo;** Piñon Nuts; Sheep Ranching; **Caldo de Cordero;** New Mexican Breakfast; Wealthy Households; silver dinner service; Patriotic Celebration; **Puches; Marquesotes; Soletas.**

Epilogue: Au Revoir and Shinin' Times   125

Index   127

Preface

In 1961, at the Denver Public Library, my wife, Betty, opened a book that contained a picture of Bent's Old Fort, an early Colorado fur-trade center built along the Santa Fe Trail. This adobe fortress, at first look, reminded one of a medieval castle. Because Betty and I were planning on building a mountain home for ourselves and had loved Santa Fe's adobe Spanish-colonial style, we were at the library, researching adobe buildings.

"Bent's Fort? How would you like to live in a place like that?" she asked.

"Let's build it," I said, not knowing how totally that would change my life.

Construction began in 1962 southwest of Denver in the foothills near Morrison, Colorado. Some 80,000 mud-and-straw adobes were made on site, each weighing 45 pounds. Timbers and vigas came from Fraser, Colorado. They were stripped and shaped with draw knives, foot adzes, and hand planes. Ten months later, we moved into the upstairs, which would be our home at The Fort. To help defray the cost, we — with no prior restaurant experience (except as eaters) — opened a 300-seat restaurant downstairs. A son and a daughter and a 500-pound pet black bear named Sissy were raised there.

Times were hard for some years, but the fascination of the Santa Fe Trail and the fur-trade period got into my blood as I tried to learn how things were back then. Knowing what people ate and drank was particulary useful, as our Fort's menu was dedicated to food and drink of the early West. To this day, Buffalo and elk continue to be specialties.

After reading some 1,800 primary and secondary reference books, diaries, and journalson the culinary customs of the frontier, I decided it was time to go back to graduate studies in western history at Denver University. Testing my mental muscle, I discovered how little I knew; so, voraciously, I read more widely to expand my horizons beyond Bent's Fort to the whole Santa Fe Trail, the California-Oregon Trail, the Missouri River fur trade, and America's abolitionist problems about to bring civil war.

Following a divorce in 1967, my life at The Fort sweetened when petite, blonde, blue-eyed Carrie came to dinner one night in 1969. We were married at dawn two years later on the huge red rock that looms ninety feet above The Fort. We joke that our marriage continues "on the rocks where it started," but nineteen years later, love blooms fresh nearly every day.

Needing a change from the restaurant after eleven years, I sold the business, and we were gone from our Fort from 1973 to 1986 when it came back to us on a foreclosure. But our interest in Bent's Fort never ceased. In 1975 and 1976, we worked on a film script and production of the National Parks Service interpretive film about Bent's Fort. As the Park Service was constructing a replica of the fort in 1976 on the original site near La Junta, Colorado, as a Bicentennial project, we were delighted to have various roles in the replication and interpretation.

In 1968, I produced a TV series on foods of the early West called "Frying Pans West," which was syndicated by PBS for the next twenty years. A cookbook of recipes from the series was widely distributed.

Across the land, there has recently been increasing interest in the Santa Fe Trail, resulting in the founding of the Santa Fe Trail Association. It's my hope that you, the reader, find pleasing this collection of historical references, recipes, and my somewhat unusual food experiences relating to the Old West and the Santa Fe Trail. It's been like thirty years of panning golden bits of information. Many pans of sand and dirt go by, but what excitement when you find a fat golden nugget of rare information! The quest, too, has brought us the pleasure of the gracious company of fine colleagues, lovers of western history.

Please, dear reader, forgive the inconsistency of having recipes two ways — narrative and modern with measurements — but often the flavor of the original recipe's old words is tastier than lists of ingredients and quantities. I have adapted most of the recipes from the old cookbooks to accommodate the twentieth-century cook in the hope that he or she will be interested in trying some of them.

In addition to supplying an index, I have included a table of contents modeled after the old 19th-century style. At the end of each chapter, I have listed not only the sources from which the recipes come but also a few other books in which the interested reader may find more detail about the subject matter. Though most of these sources have contributed to this book in various ways, they have particularly added to much of my knowledge and love of this interesting period of American history.

And now, let's saddle up!

Acknowledgments

Red roses to my family for blunting my anger and frustration while I learned a new word-processing program in the final stages of writing this book. My wife, Carrie, especially, whose strong fingers have rubbed my left-shoulder knot unendingly and who has kept me alive with early-morning four-mile walks so that I don't attach myself to the computer totally, like a vine weed. A garden of beautiful flowers to her, too, for lending her rare talents as a fine artist to this book.

Chocolate for my children, Keith and Holly, who have lent themselves as guinea pigs to a world of strange eating.

And, for my sister, Dr. Mary Arnold, whose sharp eyes and crackerjack mind found the tiny typos and misspellings, grammatical omissions, and other cracks in my perceived perfect work, lots of roses, and a big hug for her time-consuming efforts.

A hero's medal for Bill Gwaltney, the fur-trade historical interpreter who has inspired many of us to split hairs in "trying to get it right."

Much love and kisses to the Denver Public Library's western history department leader, Eleanor Gehres; and a "many thanks" for Augie, her skilled helper, who looked up the weird and the unknown. The same to the New Mexico Historical Library's team: Tom Chávez, director; Diana De Santis, curator; Orlando Romero, who tried hard to get his auntie's recipe for *puches;* and photo archivist friends Richard Rudisill and Art Olivas, who kept feeding me fascinating food-history tidbits and trivia of great value. To George Elmore at Fort Larned, many thanks for the letters and recipes. A special thanks to my friend at the National Archives, Sara Jackson, for the gift of her book — a collection of recipes prepared in 19th-century military hospitals.

A "Waugh" for our dear good friends and co-authors with us of the mountain-man toast, Peter and Mary Olch in Maryland. Fond memories of that pot of margaritas after the lectures we gave at Bent's Fort. And a gold-plated Bible for Gene Hollon, master historian, whose morality letters are historical documents that have given me the strength to go forward.

Other great helpers include David Margolis and Jean Moss, Myra Ellen Jenkins, David Lavender, Merrill Mattes, and David Weber, all of whom have helped to inspire this book.

Eating Up the Santa Fe Trail

Chapter 1

Wagons Ho!

Beginnings of the Santa Fe Trail

The historic Santa Fe Trail began in 1821 at Franklin, Missouri, a small town northwest of St. Louis. There had been some limited trade between Spanish-controlled New Mexico and the French in the Mississippi valley for more than a century. In 1792, Pedro Vial, a trusted French explorer living in Santa Fe, was directed by the city's Spanish governor to open a road to St. Louis. But because of Spanish fears of America's aggressive intentions, Americans weren't welcome in the frontier city. Military explorer Zebulon Pike and his men were jailed, as were the few trappers who stumbled into Santa Fe. After Mexican independence in 1821, however, word filtered back to Missouri that Mexico might welcome some trade.

The first true trading expedition to Santa Fe was put together that same year by William Becknell, the Franklin, Missouri, entrepreneur now termed "Father of the Santa Fe Trail." Taking samples of trade goods, Becknell arrived in Santa Fe in November 1821 and made a huge profit. Others soon followed on his heels. Eager New Mexican buyers stimulated another Becknell trip the following year, this time with covered wagons, and the Santa Fe Trail was born.

The many expeditions' packhorses and mules passed through the lush, green east Missouri countryside, rumbling into the little bustling village of Arrow Rock by the Missouri River. Later, legend has it that on his return from Mexico, Becknell emptied bags of silver dollars into the deep stone gutters in front of the Arrow Rock Tavern to dramatize the profits of the expedition. It may well have happened in Franklin, not Arrow Rock, which wasn't founded until 1829. Nonetheless, charming Arrow Rock has a long association with the

Oxbow on porch
of Hays House Hotel
Council Grove

Santa Fe Trail, Dr. John Sappington's famous malaria pills, and artists who portrayed the early days so vividly. The fine houses built there of stone and of brick speak of a quality of life rare on the early frontier. Good food, too, has long been an Arrow Rock heritage.

As far back as 1668, French Baron La Houton wrote of hunting the splendid wild turkeys at Arrow Rock, where game was plentiful due to the salt springs across the river. La Houton himself had taken a hundred of the birds.

An old story is told that Henry Nave, one of Arrow Rock's first settlers, had grown tired of the constant diet of deer, bear, and wild turkeys, so he visited a man who had some pigs. The man's wife didn't want to sell him any, but Nave finally persuaded her, trading his own wife's sidesaddle for two shoats for starting a pig farm. From that time on, pork in Arrow Rock has been more popular than beef, and "steak" on the menu more often means pork than beef. Accompanying the steaks of both varieties, traditional Arrow Rock specialties include blackberry cobbler and double-crust strawberry-rhubarb pie.

Rhubarb Stalks Pie, or Persian Apple

"Rhubarb stalks or the Persian Apple is the earliest ingredient for pies, which the Spring offers. Strip the skin and cut the stalks into small bits, and stew very tender. These are dear pies for they take an enormous quantity of sugar" (Child, The American Frugal Housewife, 69).

Other cookbooks of the period recommend against pre-stewing the rhubarb and simply suggest you fill up the pie with rhubarb pieces and strawberries, liberally sugaring it between layers of rhubarb pieces, dusting with a bit of cinnamon, perhaps a little grated lemon peel, dotting with butter nips, and covering with a top crust, with forked perforations to allow it to breathe. I personally would mix into the sugar one-half teaspoon of almond extract to compliment the strawberry and rhubarb.

T. C. Rainey tells of a dinner in Arrow Rock in early days:

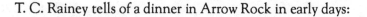

In due time, supper, not dinner, was announced, and such a meal! Baked spareribs, brown and juicy; fresh sausages; cold chicken; broiled ham of last year's vintage, with its dark red buttery gravy; potatoes; baked apples; pickles, sweet and sour; preserves, two or three varieties; comb honey, brown corn bread and biscuits hot every few minutes; a great pyramid of yellow butter; and smoking by the side of Mrs. Wood at head of the table, a pot of coffee breathing incense (Rainey, *Along the Old Trail*, 66).

Following the first successful trading trips, other merchants pursued the trail to Santa Fe. After Arrow Rock, the west-moving freight wagons would soon pass Boone's Lick, where great steaming pans of salt-spring water were boiled dry to make commercial salt, crucial to food preservation. You could find wild turkeys there, as well. Then, on to Lexington and Fort Osage, Missouri, where in the earliest days of the trail, one could stock up on bells, buttons, mirrors, tobacco twists, beads, gunpowder, and other trade goods for Indians.

The road wound west through Independence to Westport, Missouri, where in later years, 1828–1850, the great wagon trains would assemble for both the Santa Fe Trail and the California-Oregon treks. In early spring, at Westport, you'd find a polyglot of nationalities — Yankee traders from New England; French and Canadian émigrés; Spaniards and Mexicans; German political refugees; English travelers (in those days, still generally considered to be spies); blacks from both North and South — slave and free; and American Indians from many tribes. All were involved in the business of the trail.

Holding pens for the cattle, horses, mules, and oxen perfumed the air. So, too, rose both smell and din of many blacksmiths' coal-fire forges, where day and night was heard pounding of iron into wagon-wheel tires, horseshoes, and the tools of travel.

"Wagons Ho!" followed days of outfitting and planning, election of the wagon master and his lieutenants, and purchase of foodstuffs. By 1829, freighting on the Santa Fe Trail was big business. In the beginning, you could take a train of freight wagons to New Mexico loaded with manufactured steam-loom shirtings and cotton hose, woolen goods, cutlery, and looking glasses and return home to Missouri laden with silver, mules, and furs. Indeed, it's said that the famed Missouri mule actually spoke Spanish, revealing his New Mexican origins!

Emigrant travelers stocked up with basics. Each wagon might include the following: one barrel of flour; 150 pounds salt pork or bacon; 100 pounds dried corn, hulled; 25 pounds green apples or peaches; a barrel of molasses; vinegar; and a keg of beef suet as a butter substitute. Freighters traveled lighter, living on coffee, bread, salt pork, and beans or cornmeal.

Gourmet sophisticates of the period might add sardines and canned oysters, French champagne, claret, and Canary Island wine from Tenerife in order to sweeten the hardships ahead. For settlers, these luxuries were often discouraged as extra frills costing valuable space and weight. But for the freighters, these luxury items brought big dollars in Santa Fe and on down the Camino Real, the royal road to Mexico.

Catfish was the specialty of the chef at the McGee Tavern and Hotel in the center of Old Westport. The Tavern was popularly known as the Catfish House when Colonel John Harris bought it in 1846 from Allen McGee. When the log tavern burned in 1852, it was rebuilt into the current Harris House Hotel.

To Fry Catfish

Fat from salt pork is best; there should be enough to cover the fish, and hot and skimmed when the fish are laid in. Make [the fish] quite dry, and rub a little flour over it, but no salt, if you wish to have it brown well. For six pounds of fish, fry four slices of salt pork. For good plain gravy, mix two or three teaspoonsful of flour with a little water, and stir into the fat that the fish was fried in; put in a little butter, salt and pepper; if you wish to have the gravy rich, add wine, catsup and spices. Turn the gravy over the fish (Webster, The Improved Housewife, 67).

Fish should not be put in to fry until the fat is boiling hot. It is very necessary to observe this. It should be dipped in Indian [corn]meal before it is put in. People are mistaken, who think fresh fish should be put into cold water as soon as it is brought into the house; soaking it in water is injurious. If you want to keep it sweet, clean it, wash it, wipe it dry with a clean towel, sprinkle salt inside and out, put it in a covered dish and keep it on the cellar floor until you want to cook it (Child, The American Frugal Housewife, 58).

Farther down the trail, near Baldwin City, travelers reported enjoying wild strawberries. And even today, in the old ruts, wild strawberries are seen in June.

Wagon Train Messes

Once under way, the wagon train set a daily ritual for meals. Here is an account by George Bird Grinnell:

Blockhouse & Flagpole
Fort Osage, Mo.

[At daylight within the great corral,] the wagons' fires were kindled, and the mess cooks prepared a simple meal of bread, already cooked, and coffee. . . . On reaching the noon grounds [between 10 and 11 o'clock] the men had a light meal which was termed breakfast; and just before breaking camp, at about two or three in the afternoon, the principal meal of the day was served. This was called dinner, and included cooked meat and fresh-baked pan or skillet bread. Usually during the morning the hunters had killed a buffalo or antelope, and the men had this fresh meat for dinner, but along some stretches of the trail little game was to be found, and the men then lived on dried meat, of which there was always an abundance.

The men were organized into messes. Colonel [William] Bent and members of his family, or any guests who were travelling with the train, messed together, the white teamsters and the Mexicans also messed together while the Delawares and Shawnees, by preference, formed a separate mess of their own. Each man had his own quart cup and tin plate and carried his own knife in a sheath. Forks and spoons were not known. Each man marked his cup and plate, usually by scratching his initials or "mark" on them. The men of each mess chose a cook from among their own number, and after each meal every man washed his own cup and plate. The food, though simple, was wholesome and abundant. Meat was the staple, but they also had bread and plenty of coffee, and occasionally boiled dried apples and rice. Usually there was brown sugar, though sometimes they had to depend on the old-fash-ioned "long sweetening," that is[,] New Orleans molasses, which was brought out to the fort in hogsheads [a large cask] for trade to the Indians.

Bolduc House
ca. 1765

Ste. Genevieve, Mo.
1985

At two or three o'clock the herds were brought in and the train was set in motion, the journey often continuing until dark or after. . . . Two hunters, one a white man and the other either a Mexican or an Indian, accompanied the train, and each morning as soon as the wagons were ready to start they set out to look for game. Usually when the train reached the appointed camping place for the night the hunters were found there resting in the shade with a horseload of fresh meat. . . . The Delawares and Shawnees were great hunters, and almost always when the train stopped to noon and their cattle had been turned out and the meal eaten, these Indian teamsters were to be seen striding off over the prairie, each with a long rifle over his shoulder (Grinnell, *Bent's Old Fort and Its Builders*, 25–27).

On the trail in Kansas, various businesses sprang up, serving the hungry. Westbound travelers had fond memories of the ample chicken dinners with rich yellow gravy offered at the Shaker settlements in South Union, Kentucky, and in Ohio. Public houses, such as the Mahaffie House, southwest of Westport, near Olathe, often served simple but scrumptious meals of beef, ham, and chicken. Here's the famous Shaker recipe:

Shaker Chicken Fricassee

1 young roasting hen, 3 to 4
    pounds
seasoned flour
3 tablespoons clear fat
3 cups boiling water
1 bay leaf
5 peppercorns, ground
1 teaspoon summer savory
1 teaspoon tarragon
⅓ cup parsley, chopped
1 small onion, chopped
1 teaspoon each salt and
    pepper
4 tablespoons butter
4 tablespoons flour
2 egg yolks
1 cup heavy cream, heated

Cut up chicken in four pieces, wash and dry it. Roll in seasoned flour and brown to golden color in a deep pot with fat. When richly golden, add boiling water to cover, bay leaf, pepper, herbs, parsley, and onion. Cover pot and simmer till chicken is tender, 1 to 1-½ hours. Add salt and pepper.

Remove chicken from stock and keep it warm. There should be three cups of stock. In a saucepan, melt four tablespoons of butter, stir in the flour, and cook lightly. Then pour in one cup of hot stock. Simmer a moment, then add rest of stock. Simmer 10 minutes. In a bowl, beat egg yolks well, and pour hot cream over them gradually, stirring. Add to the chicken and gravy in the pot and slowly reheat. Don't allow to boil or it will curdle. The entire dish should be golden and rich in taste (Miller and Fuller, The Best of Shaker Cooking, 62–63).

The Hays House Restaurant at Council Grove, Kansas, served outstanding roast beef dinners. Here's how roasting was done in 1851:

Hays House
Council Grove, Kansas

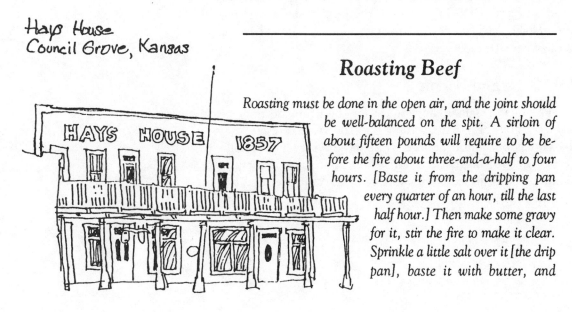

Roasting Beef

Roasting must be done in the open air, and the joint should be well-balanced on the spit. A sirloin of about fifteen pounds will require to be before the fire about three-and-a-half to four hours. [Baste it from the dripping pan every quarter of an hour, till the last half hour.] Then make some gravy for it, stir the fire to make it clear. Sprinkle a little salt over it [the drip pan], baste it with butter, and dredge it with flour. Let it go a few minutes longer, till the froth rises, then take it up and put it on the dish. Garnish it with hillocks of horseradish, finely scraped (Collins, The Great Western Cookbook, 65).

Oysters

Oysters were very popular on the Santa Fe Trail, and they came two ways: in early years of the trail, tinned, and later on, fresh. The fresh ones, from the eastern seaboard, were packed in barrels with their oyster shells opening upward so they could be fed. After reaching Iowa City, the western terminus of the railroad in 1848, oyster barrels were freighted by wagon to western towns. To keep the oysters alive and fresh, they were shipped during cool months. Barrels were packed daily with chipped ice from each stage stop's icehouse. Cornmeal was sprinkled over the top to allow the oysters to eat. As the ice melted, it carried the meal to the oysters' mouths. (This technique is still in use today.) Oysters arrived fatter and better fed than when they left the Chesapeake Bay.

Canned oysters were freighted west to Santa Fe and could be bought there even before the American invasion of 1846 during the Mexican War. Susan Magoffin, a young, nineteenth-century Kentucky bride who kept a diary of her western journey, reported eating a cold supper of oysters and champagne in Santa Fe in July 1846, in the heat of summer (Magoffin, *Down the Santa Fe Trail and Into Mexico*, 105). They had to have been canned.

Salt Pork and Bacon

The most common staple meat for the westward traveler, be he teamster or pilgrim, was salt pork, or bacon. Preserved by the salt against quick spoilage, salt pork provided a tasty addition of needed fat to the diet. When hunters on the trains found no fresh game, everyone resorted to "Old Ned," as salt pork was called. It was good eating at breakfast, at "nooning," and for supper as well.

"Old Ned" could be cut into small cubes and simmered in water with dried beans, peas, or rice as a tasty dish; or fried in the pan until crisp. With the addition of a little flour cooked into the rendered fat, and water to make a gravy, a mess boss could whip up a hearty meal with little effort.

Salt pork is too salty to eat just as it comes. It's necessary to wash out some of the salt either by soaking it in water overnight or by slicing it thin and pouring hot water over the top. With much of the saltiness removed, the crisp fried salt pork pieces are a joy to the palate.

Recipe for Salt Pork

salt pork — ¼ pound per
    person, cut into ½-inch-
    thick strips
2 tablespoons flour
salt
pepper
½ pint milk

Plan ahead. Soak the salt pork in water the night before eating it. Slice about one-quarter pound per person into one-half-inch-thick strips. Cut into bite-sized pieces. Pour two kettles of boiling water over the salt pork to remove much of the salty taste. Dry fry the salt pork pieces in a medium-hot skillet until crisp. Remove and drain on towel.

Leaving about three tablespoons of fat in the pan, add two tablespoons of flour and brown. When cooked a bit, slowly stir into the roux one-half pint milk to make a cream gravy. Add salt and pepper to taste. Catsup, wine, or spices may be added, if desired and available. Add back the crisp, fried salt pork.

Served over toast or rice, salt pork makes an easy Sunday supper, a fast lunch, or a good side dish for breakfast. Crisp fried salt pork pieces rolled in chile pepper can be served as a snack. The salty rendered fat is very good for frying fish. (Recipe collection of Sam Arnold.)

French-Canadian trappers often accompanied the trains. When the train could be stopped for a day, a favorite meal consisted of "pease porridge," or split pea soup, which took considerable time to cook.

Pois de Trappeur

Place all ingredients in a cast iron Dutch oven and bury in hot coals with lots of hot coals on top of the oven. If you have a large amount of coals, put a few shovelsful of dirt on top to hold in the heat. Leave for 6 hours, then carefully clear away dirt, and serve. In a modern kitchen, simply bake in a 300º F. oven for 2 hours. (Recipe collection of Sam Arnold.)

1 quart dried or split peas
3 quarts water
¼ pound salt pork, washed and cubed
12 black peppercorns or 2 dry hot chiles
3 bay or laurel leaves
6 or 8 juniper berries

"His Bread . . . It Was Corn Dodgers"

A frontier song's words say, "His bread was corn dodgers," and it was true throughout America; Indian cornmeal cakes were the basic staple. From the time the first settlers arrived, these grass kernels have nourished and delighted all of America. Travelers along the Santa Fe Trail were no exception. Following are some pithy, contemporary accounts of corn's use in Texas, followed by an assortment of contemporary recipes.

In 1827, Noah Smithwick, on his way from Kentucky to settle the free Texas land, stopped at Captain Jesse Burnham's place (Burnham was the first settler up the Colorado River) just as "corn was in roasting ear and the people feasting. They boiled it and fried it and roasted it, either by standing the husked ears on end before the fire and turning them till browned all around or burying them husk and all in hot ashes — the sweetest way green corn was ever cooked" (Dobie, *Tales of Old-Time Texas*, 6).

Smithwick describes the settlers punching nail holes in an old coffeepot or piece of tin that would be used as a grater or scraper for the still-milky grains of corn. Bread from the gratings was "very rich and sweet, if a bit heavy" (Dobie, 6). Scraped fresh corn makes marvelous green corn fritters.

After the meal

Green Corn Fritters

1 pint young and tender
green corn, grated
3 eggs
2 tablespoonsful milk or
cream
1 tablespoonful melted butter, if milk is used
1 teaspoonful salt

Set out ingredients in order. Beat the eggs well, add the corn by degrees, also the milk and butter, thicken with just enough flour to hold them together, adding one teaspoonful of baking powder to the flour. Have ready a kettle of hot lard, drop the corn from the spoon into the fat, and fry a light brown. They are also nice fried in butter and lard, the same as fried eggs (Gillette, The American Cookbook, 239).

A. A. Parker, Esq., wrote in his *Trip to the West and Texas* in 1834 that "even corn bread was scarce for beef could be raised with less trouble than corn" (Dobie, 6). Following Stephen F. Austin's colonization in Texas, and after he had personally acquired many thousands of acres of land, Austin wrote, "I am still very poor, living on coffee made out of parched corn, bread, milk and butter" (Dobie, 3). Even at that, Austin was better off than most, for early reports mention the great prevalence of corn bread, but no milk or butter. In 1854, Frederick Law Olmsted wrote in his *Journey Through Texas* that "morning, noon and night, food was corn bread and salt pork" (Dobie, 4).

Here are some traditional corn bread recipes with different variations, from a cookbook found in my parents' attic.

1 quart milk
1 pint cornmeal
½ cup yeast [a doughy
starter; use sourdough
starter and bread recipe]
1 teacupful wheat flour
1 teaspoonful salt
2 tablespoonsful melted butter
2 eggs, well beaten
½ teaspoonful soda

New England Corn Cake

Scald the milk and gradually pour it on the cornmeal and flour; when cool, add the butter and salt, also one-half cup of yeast. Do this at night, in the morning beat thoroughly and add two well-beaten eggs and one-half teaspoonful of soda dissolved in a spoonful of water. Pour the mixture into buttered deep earthen plates, let stand 15 minutes to rise again, then bake from 20 to 30 minutes (Gillette, 219).

Corn Bread
(St. Charles Hotel, New Orleans)

Mix the meal and flour smoothly and gradually with the milk, then the butter, molasses, and salt, then the beaten eggs; lastly, dissolve one level teaspoonful of baking soda in a little milk and beat thoroughly all together. Bake nearly 1 hour [at 375º F.] in well-buttered tins, not very shallow. This recipe can be made with sweet milk by using baking powder in place of soda (Gillette, 219).

2 cups sifted cornmeal
½ cup flour
2 cups sour milk
2 eggs, well-beaten
½ cup molasses or sugar
1 teaspoonful salt
2 tablespoonsful melted butter
1 teaspoonful baking soda

Virginia Corn Bread

Sift together the flour, cornmeal, sugar, salt, and baking powder. Rub in the cold lard; add the well-beaten eggs and then the milk. Mix into a moderately stiff batter; pour it into well-greased, shallow baking pans [pie tins are suitable]. Bake from 30 to 40 minutes (Gillette, 219).

3 cups white cornmeal
1 cup flour
1 tablespoonful sugar
1 teaspoonful salt
2 heaping teaspoonsful baking powder
1 tablespoonful cold lard
3 cups milk
3 eggs, well beaten

Boston Corn Bread

Mix ingredients, steam for 3 hours, and brown a few minutes in the oven. The same made of sweet milk and baking powder is equally good (Gillette, 220).

1 cup sweet milk
2 cups sour milk
⅔ cup molasses
1 cup wheat flour
4 cups cornmeal
1 teaspoonful soda

Indian Loaf Cake
(St. Charles Hotel, New Orleans)

1 teacupful powdered white
    sugar
1 cup rich milk
2 ounces butter
1 saltspoon salt [½ teaspoon]
yellow Indian cornmeal [½
    pound, or 2 cups]
3 eggs, beaten
1 teacupful yeast [a doughy
    starter; use sourdough
    starter and bread recipe]

Add sugar, salt, and butter to milk. Heat to scalding. Add cornmeal until a thick mush results. Beat it very hard for 15 minutes and set away to cool. Then beat three eggs very light and stir into lukewarm milk-and-corn mix. Add yeast and beat for 15 minutes more, for much of the goodness of the cake comes from being beaten long and well. Pour into a well-greased pan with a pipe in the center [Bundt or angel-food cake pan], allow to rise for 4 hours in a warm place, then bake 2 hours in a moderate oven. Serve upside down, cut in slices, with butter. Eat warm (Gillette, 220).

Johnnie Cake
(old plantation style)

1 quart Indian meal [corn-
    meal]
1 pint warm water
1 teaspoonful salt

Sift Indian meal into a pan; make a hole in the middle and pour in one pint of warm water, adding one teaspoonful of salt. With a spoon, mix the meal and water gradually into a soft dough; stir it very briskly for a quarter of an hour or more, till it becomes light and spongy. Then spread the dough smooth and evenly on a straight, flat board (a piece of the head of a flour barrel will serve for this purpose).

Place the board nearly upright before an open fire, and put an iron against the back to support it. Bake it well; when done, cut it in squares and send it hot to table, split and buttered (Gillette, 220).

EATING UP THE SANTA FE TRAIL

Spider Corn Cake

Beat eggs and sugar together. Then add one cup sweet milk and sour milk in which you have dissolved the soda. Add salt. Then mix cornmeal and flour with this. Put a spider or skillet on the range, and when it is hot, melt in two table-spoonsful of butter. Turn the spider so that the butter can run up on the sides of the pan. Pour in the corncake mixture and add one more cup of sweet milk, but do not stir afterward. Put this in the oven and bake from 20 to 35 minutes at 375º F. When done, there should be a streak of custard through it (Gillette, 221).

2 eggs
¼ cup sugar
2 cups sweet milk
1 cup sour milk
1 teaspoonful soda
1 teaspoonful salt
1-⅔ cups granulated corn-
    meal
⅓ cup flour
2 tablespoonsful butter

Southern Cornmeal Pone, or Corn Dodgers

Mix with cold water into a soft dough the cornmeal, salt, and butter or lard. Mold into oval cakes with the hands and bake in a very hot oven [400º F.] in well-greased pans. To be eaten hot. The crust should be brown (Gillette, 221).

1 quart southern cornmeal,
    sifted
1 teaspoonful salt
1 tablespoonful butter or
    lard, melted
cold water

During his western travels, A. A. Parker stopped at one-room local cabins where the families fared on corn bread, meat, and sweet potatoes. He added, "Some places . . . they had 20 or 30 cows but no butter, milk or cheese." He verified the saying that "Texas had more cows and less milk than any country on earth" (Dobie, 4).

San Jacinto Corn

One of the historic food stories told on the Santa Fe Trail about the importance of Indian corn dealt with the days after the battle of San Jacinto, Texas, April 21, 1836. Captured Mexican General Santa Anna was brought before Texas General Sam Houston. Santa Anna asked Houston how the starving Texans could expect to succeed against the well-fed Mexican troopers. Houston pulled an ear of dried corn from his pocket. Looking the Mexican general straight in the eye, Houston asked Santa Anna how he ever expected to conquer men fighting for freedom "whose general can march for four days with one ear of corn for his rations." Sam Houston's men, overhearing this, later asked for the remainder of the ear of corn, which was distributed among them grain-by-grain. Houston requested that each man take a grain home, plant it, and raise what he termed "San Jacinto Corn" to remind them of their bravery (Dobie, 10–12).

The men did, indeed, raise corn from this ear, and its name has become "Sam Houston Corn." A descendant describes the corn as "full of goodness as roasting ears, as lye hominy in the big iron pot, as pone bread in skillet, as ash cakes cooked in wet shucks over hot coals, as corn dumplings cooked with turnip greens, with pot liquor and as rocka-hominy [which was hominy corn parched, ground, and then sweetened — about the same thing as Mexican *pinole*]. Hominy was one of the most concentrated and easily carried foods known" (Dobie, 12).

Hominy, or Nixtamal

Southerners and New Englanders alike enjoyed hominy corn. On the Santa Fe Trail, it was carried dried in whole kernel or ground as "grits." Grits boiled in water cooked faster than the whole kernels and was eaten plain, fried, topped with syrup, butter, milk, sugar, or whatever made it tastier, for plain grits are blander than bland.

Hominy corn was made in this way. Every kernel of corn has a hard skin covering the soft inner meat. Indians found that this hull could be removed by boiling the corn in water and ashes. In a later method, wood ashes were placed in a trough and boiling water poured through it. The resulting leaching action produced a caustic solution that was then used for boiling the corn to remove the hulls. Today calcium hydroxide (slaked lime) is mixed with water to achieve the same effect. The resulting product was once called samp in New England, hominy in the South, and among the Mexican Indians, *nixtamal*.

The "Mexican flavor" of corn tortillas and chips comes from the lime-water flavor still remaining after the corn has lost its hull and has been washed several times. During the boiling process, the kernels become softened. Stirring releases the hulls which float to the surface and are lifted off. The corn is then dried for later use or ground into *masa* (dough) for making into tortillas. In the Southwest, the whole processed kernel is called *posole*. In many areas of the nation, one may buy posole either dry or damp or sometimes frozen. It is often used in making a soup or stew, tamales, and other recipes, which will follow in Chapter 8.

Sourdough

Most mess wagons coming west held a small keg or box of sourdough starter. It's a simple matter to begin bread by making a medium-thick starter batter of flour and warm water. Yeasts in the air simply fall upon the flour-water mix, beginning a fermentation. The batter is then left covered in a warm place.

Recipe for Sourdough Starter and Bread

There is a great mystique, developed by famous sourdough cooks, about "special wild yeasts" necessary to sourdough preparation. This is a myth. In fact, the air around us holds enough good yeast and bacteria to begin fermentation.

Simply mix one-half cup of water with hard-wheat white flour and work it well into a malleable, wet, sticky dough ball. Put it into a bowl, cover with a damp dish towel held in place with a rubber band, and leave it on a warm kitchen shelf for three days. Once it begins to swell and gives off a yeasty smell, it's ready to make bread.

This "starter," sometimes called "the chef," is then mixed with flour, water, salt, and sometimes a little fat to make a hearty bread. If you are baking eight loaves or more weekly, at each use there should be at least two cups or more of the starter left behind for the next day's batch.

Equal amounts of flour and water are re-added to the starter, filling up the container.

Bread is made by allowing the dough to "proof," or rise nearly double its size. It is then punched down, and the sponge allowed to rise once again, this time in whatever loaf form is favored — long or round or rectangular. Diagonal slashes are then cut across the loaf with a razor or sharp knife.

When risen the second time, put the dough in a 400º F. oven and bake for 15 minutes, then at 375º F. for another 20 minutes. The amount of time will depend on the kind of bread. Whole wheat, rye, and heavier breads take longer than a thin baguette. During the initial cooking, keep the surface moist to allow the bread to reach its maximum rise. A pan with water placed on an oven rack below the bread will create a crisp crust. (To simulate the commercial steam-injected ovens, I throw a handful of ice cubes onto the oven floor to make steam.)

To give the crust a sheen, paint an egg white mixed with a little water over the top before baking, or if you like a golden color, use a wash of egg yolk with a little water. This is called "endoring" (making golden) your loaf. (Recipe collection of Sam Arnold.)

To make biscuits, "Cooky" put flour in a large pan and made a hole in the center with his fingers. Into this hole, he poured several cups of the bubbly sourdough batter. Some lard, salt, and a little baking soda (called saleratus) were added to the mixture and kneaded together. The dough had to be reasonably moist and sticky and thoroughly mixed.

The cook then pinched off dough, swabbed the pieces with a coating of melted fat so they wouldn't stick together, and packed them tightly in the bottom of a cast-iron Dutch oven. The Dutch oven was then put in the coals to bake, with coals on top to brown the bread. About 30 minutes gave adequate time for the yeast dough mixed with the baking soda to rise and become a delicious bread.

Dutch ovens, in spite of their weight, were carried on wagons because of their versatility. One could fill a Dutch oven with bread or biscuits, meat or beans, birds or soup, and then bury it in hot coals. Hot coals could also be placed in the depression on the lid. The Mexicans had many recipes calling for *entre dos fuegos* (between two fires), which meant heat both below and above. A cowboy is said to have waxed poetic about the joys of these biscuits: "The old Dutch oven never failed to cook the things just right. T'was covered o'er with red hot coals and when we fetched her out, the biscuits they were of the sort no epicure would flout" (poem attributed to Arthur Chapman).

Not all frontier people liked sourdough. It was considered unhealthy and not tasty by many. In *The American Cookbook* instructions state:

> In mixing with milk, the milk should be boiled — not simply scalded, but heated to boiling over hot water, then set aside to cool before mixing. Simply heating will not prevent bread from turning sour in the rising, while boiling will act as a preventative.
>
> The yeast must be good and fresh if the bread is to be digestible and nice. Stale yeast produces instead of vinous fermentation, an acetous fermentation which flavors the bread and makes it disagreeable. If either the sponge or the dough be permitted to over-work itself; that is to say, if the mixing and kneading be neglected when it has reached the proper point for either, sour bread will probably be the consequences in warm weather and bad bread in other. Sour bread you should never eat if you desire good health (Gillette, 211).

Because wheat flour was often in scarce supply in the early days of the West, biscuits made of it were a Sunday treat. In some homes, flour biscuits were called "Billy Seldom," while the unvarying daily corn bread was termed "Johnny Constant."

Fried Bread, or Doughnuts

It is not known when fried bread first made its western appearance. Deep-fat frying was apparently unknown before the advent of the white man's metal pans. Fried bread came from Europe. Perhaps recipes for the "oily cakes" of the Dutch or Germans were picked up and used.

Olykoeks
(Oily Cakes, or Raised Doughnuts)

1 cup milk
1 package active dry yeast or
    1 cake compressed yeast
¼ cup lukewarm water
1 cup brown sugar, firmly
    packed
6 cups sifted all-purpose flour
1 teaspoon salt
1 teaspoon cinnamon or nut-
    meg
2 eggs, well beaten
1 cup softened butter
fat for deep-fat frying

Scald milk, then cool to lukewarm. Sprinkle yeast over lukewarm water to dissolve. Sift together sugar, flour, salt, and cinnamon or nutmeg. Combine milk and yeast in a large bowl. Stir in the flour with your hands (the dough will be very heavy), then stir in beaten eggs. Cover and let rise in a warm place until double in size. Punch down the dough, then work in the butter with your hands until dough is smooth and well blended. Roll about one-half-inch thick on a lightly floured board and cut with a doughnut cutter.

Place doughnuts on a tray lined with waxed paper, cover again, and let rise in a warm place until light and puffy. Drop several at a time into deep fat preheated to 375º F. on deep-fat thermometer or until a one-inch cube of bread browns in 60 seconds. Fry until nicely browned on both sides. Lift from fat, drain on paper towels, and sprinkle with confectioner's sugar, granulated sugar, or a mixture of granulated sugar and a little cinnamon. Makes about 40 (The American Heritage Cookbook, 562).

Resources and References

The American Heritage Cookbook. The American Heritage Publishing Company, Inc.; distributed by Simon and Schuster, 1964.

Becknell, William. "The Journals of Capt. Thomas Becknell from Boone's Lick to Santa Fe and From Santa Cruz to Green River." *Missouri Historical Review*, Vol. 4, No. 2 (January 1910), 65–84.

Child, Mrs. *The American Frugal Housewife*. New York: Samuel S. and William Wood, 1844.

Collins, Mrs. A. M. *The Great Western Cookbook*. New York: A. S. Barnes & Co., 1851.

Dobie, J. Frank. *Tales of Old-Time Texas*. Boston: Little, Brown & Co., 1955.

Magoffin, Susan Shelby. *Down the Santa Fe Trail and Into Mexico: The Diary of Susan Shelby Magoffin, 1846–1847*. Edited by Stella M. Drumm. New Haven, Conn.: Yale University Press, 1926.

Miller, Amy Bess, and Persis Fuller. *The Best of Shaker Cooking*. New York: Collier Books, 1976.

Parkman, Francis. *The Oregon Trail*. Garden City, N.Y.: Doubleday & Co., 1946. (There have been many editions of this book, but the original was written in the 1840s. Descriptions of Westport are in Chapter 1.)

Rainy, T. C. *Along the Old Trail*. Vol. 1. Marshall, Mo.: Marshall Chapter DAR, 1914 (references to Baron La Houton, 23; Henry Nave, 26; dinner at Arrow Rock, 66).

Rittenhouse, Jack D. *The Santa Fe Trail: A Historical Bibliography*. Albuquerque: University of New Mexico Press, 1986.

Webster, Mrs. A. L. *The Improved Housewife, or Book of Receipts*. Hartford, Conn.: Ira Webster, 1843.

Chapter 2

Thirst on the Trail

Cups of Java, or How to Make Coffee

In the early days of the Santa Fe Trail, coffee was sold in its green unroasted state:

> Green coffee beans are virtually indestructible, and retain their flavor almost indefinitely. Dry them first in an iron pot, over a moderate fire, for some hours before they are roasted. Hang the pot so high as not to burn it. After drying three or four hours, place it on a hot bed of coals, and stir it constantly until roasted enough which is determined by biting one of the lightest colored kernels. If brittle, pronounce the whole done. Put into two or three pounds a bit of butter as big as a walnut, before taking it off. Box it tight immediately to keep in the steam [to save the coffee's aroma] (Webster, 172).

Just after the Civil War, the Pittsburgh firm of Arbuckle Bros. developed a method of coating roasted beans. Arbuckle's sprayed its beans with a thin film of egg white and sugar syrup, which sealed in the roasted flavor oils and prevented oxidation. No longer did the trail cook have to spend minutes carefully watching the exact degree of pan roasting to prevent burning the coffee beans.

Here's an old-timers' recipe for campfire coffee (yes, you actually crush up a whole egg — shell and all — into the grounds):

Camp Fire Coffee

Heat a pot of cold water to boiling. [Allow to boil only 2 to 3 minutes.] Place a cup of ground coffee and an egg in the middle of a piece of cheesecloth and tie the cheesecloth into a sack. Then break the egg in the sack and mix with the coffee by massaging the bag. Drop the sack into the boiling water and cook for 4 minutes. Add one-half cup cold water to settle any grounds. The coffee is absolutely superb. (Recipe collection of Sam Arnold.)

2 quarts cold water
1 egg
1 cup ground roasted coffee
½ cup cold water

Tea, Herbal Teas, and Hot Chocolate

Wagoneers, teamsters, freighters, and military personnel carried India, Ceylon, and China tea with them. Darjeeling, Yung Hyson, and Souchong teas were seen in various inventories, and it's possible that along the trail these teas were drunk more often than coffee. Tea was certainly easier to prepare, requiring no roasting or grinding. Tea leaves were stored either loose in chests or sometimes in hard, slab-like blocks.

In 1849, with cholera dropping people in their tracks along the Santa Fe Trail, tea, with its astringent tannic qualities, became ever more popular. A common remedy for diarrhea, a symptom of cholera, called for taking doses of strong tea from both directions. A tea made from the tannic bark of the choke-cherry bush found along many parts of the trail was also commonly used to treat diarrhea. Pipsissewa, originally a Cree Indian herb used to break up kidney stones, was grown by the Shaker communities. Its astringent tea was used as a tonic and diuretic. Indians called it pipsissewa "love in winter." Mormon Tea (*ephedra* spp.) was used as a mild decongestant.

In the mid-nineteenth century, chocolate was a popular drink and found its way over the Santa Fe Trail. Here's Mrs. A. L. Webster's recipe:

Recipe for Hot Chocolate

*Allow to each square, or spoonful, of fine scraped choco-
late, about a pint of water; boil from 15 to 20 minutes,
then add cream or milk, and sugar to the taste, and boil it,
uncovered, about 10 minutes longer (Webster, 174).*

Whiskey, Belly Washes, and Aguardientes

Although Cincinnati, Ohio, was America's number-one
alcohol-producing city before the Civil War, the sources for
whiskey in the West were many; it was not against the law to
build or own a still. In a letter dated February 13, 1826, Taos
trader and distiller William Workman wrote to his brother
David in Franklin, Missouri, asking for two 80-gallon stills to
be sent from St. Louis, where in the 1830s still-makers such as
John Byrd produced copper versions of various sizes for anyone
with the money. Over the years, many stills were brought to
New Mexico, where U.S. federal law did not extend. It was far
more profitable for the farmer growing grain to take his product
to market as alcohol, rather than transporting bushels of grain.
A horse could easily transport twenty-four bushels of grain
condensed into two kegs of whiskey slung across its back.

Santa Fe Trail Trader
John Luzader

The Pennsylvania Germans made rye-based Allegheny
Whiskey (named for the Allegheny River, which at Pittsburgh
joins the Monongahela River to form the Ohio River) and the
Monongahela Whiskey that gained some popularity on the
western frontier, but it was bourbon whiskey that accrued
international fame. A mixture of corn and rye whiskies
aged in charred oak barrels, bourbon derived its name
from Bourbon County, Kentucky, where most of the
whiskey is still produced. While bourbon is known as
Kentucky Whiskey, Bourbon County was originally part
of Virginia, which stretched westward to include present-day Kentucky. Later, Virginia was split into Virginia
and West Virginia, which included Bourbon County.
Still later, Kentucky was formed from a part of West
Virginia. Bourbon County originally covered a big area of
the new state. But over the years, many other counties

have been formed, and Bourbon County today comprises only a small piece of Kentucky. But the fame of "bourbon" whiskey continues to spread worldwide.

Before the 1846 American invasion of New Mexico, Mexican customs officials wrote up lists of items found on the wagons arriving at Santa Fe. They wrote them phonetically in Spanish. Hence, Kentucky and Tennessee whiskey became "Quentoque y Tenaysi Juisque."

In the first decades of the nineteenth century, alcoholism and drunkenness increased greatly to create a major national problem. Powerful temperance groups sprang up and decimated existing apple orchards with axes to slow down applejack production. Temperance-minded voters elected representatives who passed anti-alcohol legislation designed to stop the debauchery of both white and Indian. One law, passed in the 1820s, prohibited the sale of whiskey to the Indians in the West.

Liquor Barrel

In 1822, only a small amount of alcohol — for personal use, not trade — could be legally taken west by travelers. It was not long, however, before the law was abused and circumvented, with trappers and traders carrying fifty gallons or more per man "for individual private use." In 1832, a new law, enforced by armed military inspectors, mandated stricter prohibition of alcohol importation into Indian country. There was a major inspection station just outside of Fort Leavenworth on the Missouri River. Other stations along waterways and trails winding west served as federal checkpoints. Stills, however, were smuggled into Indian country and erected at the private fur-trade forts. Fort Union (of the north) in North Dakota operated a successful still for a few years before a disgruntled man blew the whistle to the federals.

Restrictions may have slowed the whiskey trade to the Indians, but it was never stopped. Competing with the Canadians, the American fur firms were at a distinct disadvantage. The Canadian-based Hudson's Bay Company and Northwest Company had no such prohibitions on trading alcohol, and many Indians consequently gave their fur business to those two firms. In retaliation, whiskey was smuggled west, sometimes distilled illegally, and often brought north from distilleries in New Mexico during Mexican rule.

Whiskey, as is true with all distilled spirits, is clear when it comes out of the still. It was several years before the Civil War, however, that the use of burnt-sugar caramel coloring came into vogue, and since that time, whiskey has been colored, either by caramel or coloration that comes from the charred wooden barrels in which it is aged.

In Philadelphia, E. C. Booz produced bottles shaped like little houses, with his name and the year, 1840, blown in the glass. He was perhaps the first whiskey-maker who directly marketed his products under his own distinctive glass bottle. Prior to that time, whiskey was usually sold in barrels.

Wholesale whiskey vendors would often provide the tavern with a supply of interesting fancy flasks and bottles, hoping that the tavern owner would fill them with the vendor's liquor. These bottles would be placed on the bar where customers could say, "I'll have me a drink from that corncob" (or hat, cornucopia, shoe, log cabin, canteen, violin and bull fiddle). (One is reminded of the fancy Jim Beam decanters of today.)

The alcohol that came west for the Indian trade despite federal efforts to limit or eliminate it was variously termed "Great Father's Milk," belly wash, and whistle-belly vengeance. Traders often watered down the rectified alcohol to extend its profitability. Many additives, including tobacco, red peppers, black gun powder and sometimes laudanum (opium tincture), were used to give some interesting taste.

Modern consumers of the following recipe (more than two hundred liters were served at my restaurant in 1989) find "Injun" whiskey (without laudanum) both tasty and smooth, far preferable to regular raw whiskey.

1 cup water
2 tablespoons cut tobacco
4 small dried red peppers
½ teaspoon black
    gunpowder (DO NOT
    USE MODERN HIGH-
    SPEED POWDER, WHICH
    IS POISONOUS!)
1 liter Old Crow or similar
    bourbon whiskey

Injun Whiskey

Boil tobacco and red peppers for 5 minutes. Strain, retaining the tea. Add this to the whiskey, little by little, to taste. Then add gunpowder. It should have a gentle nip from the peppers and an herbal taste from the tobacco. The small amount of saltpeter in the black powder will have no effect! (Arnold, Frying Pans West, 53.)

At Bent's Fort on the Santa Fe Trail, near present-day La Junta, Colorado, the "hailstorm" was the traditional Fourth of July libation. Made with wild mint (yerba buena), sugar, whiskey, and ice from the icehouse, the hailstorm recipe will be found in Chapter 6.

Although Pauillac and St. Julian Medoc wines were also served at Bent's Fort and champagne was freighted along the Santa Fe Trail (Susan Magoffin drank it in Santa Fe in the summer of 1846), most drinkers preferred eastern whiskey, Pass Whiskey — the grape brandy from El Paso — or Taos Lightning.

By 1846, there were at least six distilleries operating in the Taos area, making a clear whiskey that found enthusiasts all along the Santa Fe Trail. Mexicans called it *aguardiente* (a term for any distilled spirit, coming from the Latin, *aqua vitae*, or water of life). Mountain men used the bastardization, "awardenty." More highly prized than whiskey, however, were the bottles it came in. Not just the fancy blown-glass commemorative bottles, but any glass bottle. In *Down the Santa Fe Trail and Into Mexico,* Susan Magoffin writes, in the summer of 1846, that one could buy a bottle of spirits in St. Louis for two bits ($0.25), drink the contents, and sell the empty in New Mexico for four bits ($0.50) (Magoffin, 153).

Cocktails

From Westport to Santa Fe, drinks were generally straight and simple. But early in the 1800s, the use of a few drops of bitters became highly popular. Cognac with Peychaud, Angostura, Stoughton's, or Hostetter's bitters, stirred with a rooster feather, was termed a "cock tail," and some believe this may be where that term for a mixed drink originated. A particularly delicious bitters was invented by a French refugee apothecary named Peychaud, who escaped from San Domingo during the 1798 revolution and brought the recipe with him to New Orleans. It was the basis of many "cocktails" and is *the* bitters to use in a "Sazerac" cocktail. While Peychaud is not nearly as well known as famed Angostura bitters, it is still made today by the Sazerac Company in New Orleans.

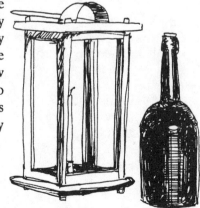

THIRST ON THE TRAIL

¼ ounce French *pastis* (an anise-flavored spirit such as absinthe, Pernod, or Ricard)
2 ounces cognac (some use bourbon whiskey)
1 teaspoon fine sugar
2 squirts Peychaud bitters
3 cubes ice

Sazerac

Wash a "rocks" glass with the pastis, up over the walls of the glass, swirled around. Add liquor and sugar. Stir well to dissolve sugar. Add bitters and ice. Serve. (Recipe collection of Sam Arnold.)

New Mexico Pot Still

made in St. Louis

Brought over the Santa Fe Trail

to make Taos Lightning

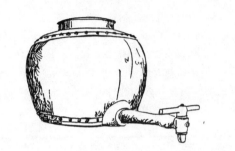

In 1862, Dr. Jerry Thomas, formerly principal bartender at the New York Metropolitan Hotel and the famed Planter's House in St. Louis, wrote *Bartender's Guide*. He lists the Martinez gin cocktail as follows:

1 dash Boker's bitters [substitute Peychaud bitters]
2 dashes maraschino liqueur
1 pony [3 ounces] gin
½ wine glass vermouth [2 ounces white vermouth]
2 small lumps ice

Martinez Gin Cocktail

Shake up thoroughly and strain into a large cocktail glass. Put a quarter of a slice of lemon in the glass and serve (Thomas, Bartender's Guide, *25).*

At the United States Hotel in Santa Fe in 1848, such a "gin cocktail" was served to writer George Brewerton by "Long Eben," the down-easter who kept the flea-ridden hotel where La Fonda stands today.

The following recipes are from the *Bartender's Guide*:

Hot Brandy and Rum Punch (for a party of fifteen)

Rub the sugar over the lemons until it has absorbed all the yellow part of the skins, then put the sugar into a punch bowl. Add the ingredients together, pour over them the boiling water, stir well, and serve. Allow one quart for four persons. [Since loaf sugar is hard to find, peel skin from lemons with a potato peeler and in a food processor or blender, combine sugar and peels. Do not use white portion of lemon peel.] (Thomas, 76.)

1 quart Jamaica rum
1 quart cognac brandy
1 pound white loaf sugar
4 lemons
3 quarts boiling water
1 teaspoonful nutmeg

The Real Georgia Mint Julep

Place mint in tumbler, add the sugar, having previously dissolved it in a little water, then the brandy, and lastly fill up the glass with shaved ice. Stir with a spoon but do not crush the mint. [This is the genuine method of concocting a Southern mint julep, but whiskey may be substituted for brandy, if preferred.] (Thomas, 29.)

1 teaspoonful white powdered sugar
¾ wine glass [3 ounces] cognac brandy
¾ wine glass peach brandy
About 12 sprigs of the tender shoots of mint

Rum

During colonial days and the early nineteenth century, rum was the favored American alcohol. Its production in the West Indies dates back at least to the early sixteenth century. Rum was found on the Swedish warship *Wasa*, which sank in Stockholm harbor in 1628 on its maiden trip. Tall, square, metal rum bottles were recovered from the wreck when the ship was raised, virtually intact, in 1961!

Sugarcane production in the West Indies was part of the three-cornered slave trade. Slaves from Africa were traded to the Indies for rum. The rum, made from sugarcane, was then taken to New England or England, where it was exchanged for trade goods. These goods were then shipped back to Africa, where they were used to purchase more slaves.

Altogether, there are about a dozen types of rum: Barbados, Cuban, Demerara, Habanero, Haitian, Jamaican, London Dock Jamaican, Martinique, New England, Philippine Islands, Puerto Rican, Venezuelan, and Virgin Islands. To make rum, sugar-rich molasses was allowed to ferment into a "wine." This bubbling, roiling, highly odorous fermentation was then distilled to make rum. In the process of boiling off, some of the alcohol-containing vapor carried with it molasses flavors, giving the rum its familiar taste. Frequently, the distillate had the additional flavor of barks, roots, and spices. Perhaps the most notable flavored rum is Demerara, named for the town on the north coast of South America. Most Demeraras are higher proof than other rums, sometimes running as high as 160 proof. Fruit extracts are sometimes used, but flavoring tinctures are generally preferred. Oak leaves, various barks, and roots are soaked in alcohol, yielding the tincture.

Cuban rum, distilled from sugarcane juice with no additives, has a very light, sweet flavor. It is quite unlike the Demerara, which has a dry, burned, deliciously spicy flavor and possesses the same aromatic and pungent flavor as the Jamaican rums much appreciated by American connoisseurs. Jamaica was also the source of the famous London Dock rums, which were shipped to London for aging. The generally cold winters in England provided an ideal place for rum aging. London Dock aged rums are considered better than those aged an equal amount of time in Jamaica. Martinique rums are heavier than the light rums of Puerto Rico and Cuba but lighter than the full-bodied, sugary Jamaicas and Demeraras.

The New England rum industry still flourishes, using molasses brought from cane sources in the Caribbean such as Puerto Rico, the Virgin Islands, and in former times, Jamaica. Puerto Rico is the largest exporter of rum to the United States. Since Puerto Rican rum is duty-free, it costs less than those from Jamaica and other foreign nations.

While Jerry Thomas, American history's most famous bartender, is supposed to be the originator of the Tom & Jerry, he makes no claim for it in his book. This spiced rum-and-egg mixture was advertised in Santa Fe on January 8, 1848, by Hartley & Powers, operators of a "bar room and grocery . . . a saloon in which can be had all kinds of liquors. Hot whiskey punch, Tom & Jerry, rum punch, as well as oyster suppers, sardines" (*Santa Fe Republican*).

Tom & Jerry
[according to Jerry Thomas]

Beat the whites of the eggs to a stiff froth, and the yolks until they are thin as water, then mix together and add the spice and rum, stir up thoroughly, and thicken with sugar until the mixture attains the consistency of a light batter. A teaspoonful of cream of tartar will prevent the sugar from settling to the bottom of the mixture. How To Serve: Take one tablespoonful of the above mixture, plus one wine glass of brandy.

Fill the glass with boiling water, grate a little nutmeg on top, and serve with a spoon. Adepts at the bar sometimes employ the following mixture: one half brandy, one quarter Jamaican rum, one quarter Santa Cruz rum. For convenience, these proportions are mixed and kept in a bottle, and a wine glassful used to each tumbler of Tom & Jerry, instead of brandy plain (Thomas, 51).

12 fresh eggs (use punch bowl for the mixture)
½ small bar glass Jamaican rum
1-½ teaspoons cinnamon
½ teaspoon ground cloves
½ teaspoon ground allspice
sufficient fine white sugar

Rocky Mountain Punch
(for a mixed party of twenty, from a recipe of Major James Foster)

Pack your punch bowl in ice in a larger bowl. Add ingredients together, add champagne just before serving, and garnish with slices of oranges and lemons (Thomas, 77).

5 bottles champagne
1 quart Jamaica rum
1 pint of maraschino [liqueur]
6 lemons, sliced
sugar to taste

Applejack

Applejack was second only to rum in popularity in colonial days and some historians even believe it surpassed rum in popularity at the beginning of the nineteenth century. Easy to make, applejack could be procured by allowing a keg of hard cider to freeze during a winter cold snap. The water would solidify, but the alcohol remained liquid. Thus, one could draw off a highly potent applejack without heat distillation. Of course, serious applejack producers used stills.

Shrubs

Shrubs were a favorite drink during the days of the Santa Fe Trail. Susan Magoffin reports drinking refreshing shrubs en route to Santa Fe. They were made by using a concentrate of berry or fruit, sweetened, often mixed with alcohol to prevent fermentation, and then mixed with water. Shrubs were often made of cherry, raspberry, or currant juice, boiled with sugar. Two or three ounces of brandy or some other spirit were added to each eight ounces of the syrup. The syrup was then added in small amounts to cool water, making a most refreshing drink for travelers on the trail.

Raspberry Shrub (to make one gallon)

8 ounces brandy
1 quart vinegar
3 quarts red raspberries
8 pounds sugar

Mix vinegar and berries together. After letting stand a day, strain it, adding to each pint one pound of sugar, and skim it clear, while boiling about half an hour. Put a wine glass [4 ounces] of brandy to each pint of the shrub when cool. Two spoonsful of this mixed with a tumbler of water is an excellent drink in warm waters and in fevers (Thomas, 63).

Rum Shrub
(to make nearly four gallons)

Mix together all but the milk, and let them remain closely covered overnight. Next day, boil the milk, and when cold, add to the mixture. Filter through a flannel bag lined with blotting paper [a coffee filter will do], and bottle, corking immediately. Serve over ice (Thomas, 63).

3 gallons best Jamaican rum
1 quart orange juice
1 pint lemon juice
6 pounds powdered sugar,
    dissolved in water
3 pints fresh milk

References

Beveridge, N. E. *Cups of Valor.* Harrisburg, Penn.: Stackpole Books, 1968.

Carson, Gerald. *The Social History of Bourbon.* New York: Dodd, Mead & Company, 1963.

Grinnell, George Bird. *Bent's Old Fort and Its Builders.* Wichita: Kansas Historical Society, 1912.

Jenkins, Myra Ellen, New Mexico Archives. Conversation with author (reference to Kentucky and Tennessee whiskey).

Magoffin, Susan Shelby. *Down the Santa Fe Trail and Into Mexico: The Diary of Susan Shelby Magoffin, 1846–1847.* Edited by Stella M. Drumm. New Haven, Conn.: Yale University Press, 1926.

Thomas, Jerry. *Bartender's Guide.* New York: Dick and Fitzpatrick, 1862.

Van Tramp, John C. *Prairie and Rocky Mountain Adventures.* Columbus: Gilmore and Rush, 1866. (Originally from writings of George Brewerton.)

Webster, Mrs. A. L. *The Improved Housewife, or Book of Receipts.* Hartford, Conn.: Ira Webster, 1843.

"William Workman Letter." Edited by David J. Weber. *New Mexico Historical Review*, April 1966, 155–161.

Chapter 3

Meeting the Buffalo on the Prairie

A Santa-Fe-Trail wagon train west was an exciting adventure for seventeen-year-old Lewis Garrard. Coming with Ceran St. Vrain, the famous Santa Fe Trail trader, in the summer of 1846, the young man first marveled at the different Indians at Westport, Missouri, the jumping-off point for the trail to Mexico. Every night the French Canadian teamsters would sing their "sweet simple music, their beautiful and piquant songs in the original language . . . it fell most harmoniously on the ear as we lay wrapped in our blankets. I used to lie admiring the bright stars until overpowered by sleep" (Garrard, *Wah-To-Yah and the Taos Trail*, 11). How fortunate we are today that this teen-age adventurer kept meticulous notes about the people and events of that time and the frontier foods they ate, many of which were quite unlike any he had known before. Here are some of his observations about buffalo:

> We never eat but twice a day, very often but once in twenty-four hours, at which scarcity of food, of course, there was grumbling. [A fellow traveler with Garrard said,] 'Darn this way of living, anyhow; a feller starves a whole day like a mean coyote and when he does eat, he stuffs himself like a

Grazing Buffalo

snake that's swallowed a frog, and is no account for an hour after.' [Garrard noted that] it was about the truth, for our ravenous hunger scarcely knew bounds (Garrard, 19).

After the first buffalo hunt, Garrard watched the men skin and butcher a

fine, fat young male. The men ate the liver raw, with a slight dash of gall by way of zest, which[,] served a la Indian, was not very tempting to cloyed appetites; but to hungry men, not at all squeamish, raw warm liver with raw marrow, was quite palatable. Before the buffalo range was half traversed, I liked the novel dish pretty well (Garrard, 19).

The young man enjoyed the warm comradeship of his companions on the wagon train, all of whom would gather for a hearty meal of "buffler." He wrote:

Good humor reigned triumphant throughout the camp. Canadian songs of mirth filled the air; and, at every mess fire, pieces of meat were cooking *en appolas:* that is, on a stick sharpened, with alternating fat and lean meat, making a delicious roast. . . . '[B]oudins' [intestines in which is contained the chyme, or grass just beginning in digestion] were roasting without any previous culinary operation but the tying of both ends, to prevent the fat, as it was liquified[,] from wasting; and when pronounced 'good' by the hungry, impatient judges, it was taken off the hot coals, puffed up with the heat and fat, the steam escaping from little punctures, and coiled on the ground or on a not particularly clean saddle blanket, looking for all the world like a dead snake.

Buffalo Cow

The fortunate owner shouts "Hyar's the doin's and hyar's the coon as savvys 'poor bull' from 'fat cow'; freeze into it, boys!" And all fall to with ready knives, cutting off savory pieces of this exquisitely appetizing prairie product.

At our mess fire there was a whole side of ribs roasted. When browned thoroughly, we handled the long bones, and as the generous fat dripped on our clothes, we heeded it not, our minds wrapped up with the one absorbing thought of satisfying our relentless appetites; progressing in the work of demolition, our eyes closed with ineffable bliss. Talk of an emperor's table . . . why, they could imagine nothing half so good! One remarkable peculiarity is there about buffalo meat . . . one can eat even beyond plenitude without experiencing any ill effects (Garrard, 28–29).

Buffalo en Appolas

Skewer bite-sized pieces of buffalo meat, putting fat between lean. Swab with oil (rendered kidney fat is best), broil over hot coals, then sprinkle with salt and red pepper. (Hump is tough and fatty, but best for high energy requirements.) The tender "fleece" meat, on the sides of the hump, now that's eatin'! (Recipe collection of Sam Arnold.)

When buffalo were killed on the prairie, there was a science to the killing. The biggest, most powerful buffalo bulls led the herd, and the young cows followed in the middle-front of the herd, protected by the lead bulls and the lesser bulls around the sides, while the old cows straggled behind. So, for the buffalo hunter, the tough job was to get at the young cows (the best eating) right in the middle-front of the herd. The skills necessary to obtain this young cow meat distinguished the professional hunter from the amateur.

A dressed-out (butchered) fifteen-month- or two-year-old bison will weigh between 500 and 600 pounds. The old bulls may weigh as much as 3,000 pounds. They may make good trophies, but they don't provide the tasty, tender eating that young bulls and cows do. The best meat I've ever tasted was from an eleven-month-old cow, grain-fed at Bent's Fort.

Mexican Buffalo Hunters

Mexican buffalo hunters were called *ciboleros*. Wearing flat straw hats, leather pants, and leather jackets, these meat hunters ranged across northeast New Mexico seeking the bison for its meat and hide. For two centuries, the buffalo-hide and -robe business with old Mexico had been a valuable revenue source for New Mexico. In records of the expeditions to Mexico in the 1840s, before the American invasion, virtually every wagon train carried quantities of hides southward.

Most ciboleros carried a quiver of bow and arrows. They also carried a long lance, rather in the fashion of a picador at a bullfight. The handle of the lance was set in a case and suspended by the horse's side with a strap from the pommel of the saddle — the point waving high over the cibolero's head. A tassel of gay, many-colored ribbons often hung at the edge of the scabbard. A few ciboleros carried guns, also with the butt in a case and the muzzle upward, corked with a fantastically tassled stopper. Even in the 1840s, guns were a luxury rarely found among the poor Mexicans. Matchlocks were still in use, although they had been obsolete in Europe for more than one hundred years, having been replaced with flintlocks and, later, percussion caps.

Josiah Gregg's *Commerce of the Prairies* describes a visit to a cibolero's camp:

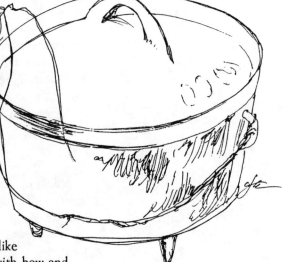

Dutch Oven
Used on the Santa Fe Trail
Delgado Family Collection
Mus. of N M

[He] afterwards brought us an abundance of dry buffalo beef, and some bags of coarse oven-toasted loaves, a kind of hard bread much used by Mexican travelers. It is prepared by opening the ordinary leavened rolls, and toasting them brown in an oven. Though exceedingly hard and insipid while dry, it becomes not only soft but palatable when soaked in water — or better still in hot coffee. But what we procured on this occasion was unusually stale and coarse, prepared expressly for battle with the Comanches, in case [the American travelers] should meet any; yet bread was bread, emphatically, with us just then.

. . . Every year, large parties of New-Mexicans, some provided with mules and asses, others with *carretas* or truckle-carts and oxen, drive out into these prairies to procure a supply of buffalo beef for their families. They hunt, like the wild Indians, chiefly on horseback, and with bow and arrow, or lance, with which they soon load their carts and mules. They find no difficulty in curing their meats even in mid-summer, by slicing it thin and spreading or suspending it in the sun; or, if in haste, it is slightly barbequed. During the curing operation they often follow the Indian practice of beating or kneading the slices with their feet, which they contend contributes to its preservation.

Here the extraordinary purity of the atmosphere is remarkably exemplified. The caravans cure meat in the same simple manner, except the process of kneading. A line is stretched from corner to corner on each side of a wagon-body, and strung with slices of beef, which remains from day to day till it is sufficiently cured to be stacked away. This is done without salt, and yet it very rarely putrifies. In truth, as blow-flies are unknown here, there is nothing to favor putrification.

. . . Caravans sometimes lay by a day or two to provide a supply of meat; when numbers of buffalo are slaughtered, and the flesh "jerked" or slightly barbequed, by placing it upon a scaffold over a fire. The same method is resorted to by Mexicans when the weather is too damp or cloudy for the meat to dry in the open air (Gregg, *Commerce of the Prairies*, Vol.1, 46–47).

By the early 1840s, buffalo were disappearing along the Santa Fe Trail. In letters written in the late 1840s, Thomas Fitzpatrick, Indian agent at Bent's Fort, pointed out that they were nearly gone in the Arkansas River valley, and he foretold that the ruination of the Indian would soon follow the disappearance of their buffalo.

Buffalo Jerky, or Carne Seca

After a kill, hunters would traditionally feast upon the fresh, choice parts: the tongue; the "fleece" — a fatty meat strip on each side of the hump backbone area; the rib racks; liver; and kidneys. The balance of the meat was taken back to the nearest fort, if it was within a few hours' ride. Otherwise, the meat was cut in long, thin strips and hung out in the air to dry, or jerk, as they called it. Instead of spoiling, it became almost permanently preserved and could travel with the hunters.

Good buffalo jerky is delicious but hard to find. Whether you have buffalo, deermeat, elk, antelope, or beef, here's the procedure for making truly delicious jerky:

Preparing Carne Seca, or Jerky

Jerky sticks are available at many bars, but the extruded ersatz jerky produced commercially in this country is not worthy of the name. Be sure you have real beef or buffalo slices that have been dried. You can easily do this yourself by having the butcher thinly slice a beef or buffalo rump. Some people dip it momentarily into lime or lemon juice and salt, then leave it hanging from a wire or over a string overnight. A bit of cheesecloth will keep away the insects, if you are finicky.

I make great jerky in my oven, but *without* any heat. Oil the racks or spray with a non-stick oil. Leave the meat strips hanging down over the metal racks. Don't let the pieces touch or overlap. You may sprinkle the pieces with salt, pepper, chile, or hot sauce if you like. Place a running electric fan on the open oven door and aim it into the oven overnight. REMEMBER . . . NO HEAT in the oven — it changes the taste. In the morning, you'll have excellent air-dried jerked meat. Use it as is, fry it, or roast it a bit in a hot oven. Toasted jerky tastes a bit like bacon and may be used in many dishes.

Marrow Bones

Nothing equals the wonderful flavor of broiled buffalo marrow. Ask your butcher to obtain some buffalo femurs and cut off the knobs with a saw, then run the bones through the saw lengthwise, exposing the marrow. Wipe away the bone dust and broil. Turn face down under overhead broiler for 6 minutes to heat the bone, then turn marrow-side up and broil for another 4 to 5 minutes. The marrow should be cooked, golden brown, but not totally liquified. Dust with salt and pepper.

Serve with toast. Using a marrow scoop or a knife, remove marrow and spread it on the toast, as you would butter. It's so delicious that my restaurant serves more than two tons of buffalo marrow bones annually. The mountain men called it "prairie butter."

While buffalo upper intestine was frequently enjoyed with the chyme (chewed grass filling) intact, as described by Garrard, other mountain men reported chopping buffalo meat into pieces and stuffing them into a long piece of cleaned, washed intestine. With the occasional addition of salt and red or black pepper to the meat, these simple sausages were termed "boudies" by the American mountain men.

Boudins

In the nineteenth-century novel *Edward Warren*, one of the characters describes a meal of stuffed buffalo-intestine sausage:

> "Let us have some boudins, boys," said the ever-active Smith. "Whar's the tender loin, aye, here it is . . ." He set them all to work. If there is nothing in that country so good as these puddings, neither is there any thing more easily cooked. Everyone had a pile of meat cut half the size of dice; Jim had his in long thin strings, cut with the grain, in the Indian fashion. The other heaps were put together and crammed into the gut, as it was turned inside out, and tied with a whang at regular intervals, so that, when cut into portions, it should not lose the juice. This was set to boil, while the delicious hump-rib was set up to roast (Stewart, *Edward Warren*, 92).

Though boudins in France are blood sausages, or "puddings" cooked in casings, French-Canadian trappers used the same term for the stuffed buffalo-intestine sausages. Americans, unable to pronounce "boudin," called them "boudies."

Buffalo Tongue

"I, by good luck, had some buffalo tongue in my pocket, that added not a little to our rural repast" (*Abert's New Mexico Report*, 45).

Considered a holy meat by the Indians, buffalo tongue was thought by many to be the greatest gourmet delicacy of the American nineteenth century. The intense flavor and fine texture, somewhat like a fine pâté, are superb and far exceed that of beef tongue, which has a coarser quality. Buffalo tongue was served at such fine hostelries as the Maxwell House and famed Delmonico's in New York City, where President Ulysses

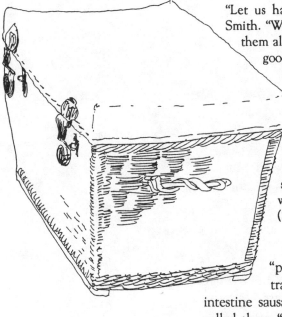

Provision Hamper
Used on the Santa Fe Trail
by E. Rosenwald, Las Vegas, New Mexico

Museum of New Mexico

S. Grant and singer Jenny Lind, the Swedish Nightingale, were reported to have feasted upon the delicacy. The demand for buffalo tongue was a major reason for the wholesale slaughter of the bison. Whole herds were killed for their hides and tongues, which were smoked, salted, or pickled, and sent east in fully-loaded railroad cars. A greenhorn [newcomer] hunter who killed a buffalo was expected to bring the tongue back to camp as a trophy. Today, in limited numbers, buffalo tongues are once again gracing gourmet palates. Fortunately, few of the public know how good they are.

Cooking a Buffalo Tongue

Slowly boil buffalo tongues about 4 hours in water flavored with a few bay leaves, some black peppercorns, and minced onion. When soft, cool and peel away the skin with a knife. Cut one-half-inch thick slices and serve hot or cold. A nice but not historic sauce I favor consists of mayonnaise, capers, horseradish, and Worcestershire sauce, to taste. (Recipe collection of Sam Arnold.)

Both moose and buffalo nose were eaten by Indians and mountain men. For the French trappers, moose nose was called "mouffle," and it had many fans. To cook a moose nose, follow this recipe:

Moose Nose

Impale the cut end of the nose on a sharp stick or steel rod. Build a steady fire and singe off the heavy dark hair thoroughly. Turn it like a giant marshmallow until all the hair is burnt. Soak it overnight in salted water. Brush with a wire brush the next day to remove all burnt residue. Cut into large pieces to reveal the inner sinus cavities. You will see some inner hair growing there. Either use a gas torch or hold the nose over an open stove flame to burn this hair off, too. Wash in salt water and brush with a wire brush till clean.

Boil the nose pieces with an onion, bay leaf, vinegar, and peppercorns for about 6 hours, adding hot water to keep it submerged. Remove, reassemble pieces into nose shape, and place on platter. Refrigerate. The juices will jell into aspic. Though the nose is mostly cartilage, with some meat here and there, boiling in acidic vinegar will soften the tissue. One may then slice thinly and serve with a piquant chile sauce and sliced lemon, as the nose is bland (though the cartilage is pleasantly crunchy). The taste is similar to a pickled pig's foot. Buffalo nose may be prepared using the same technique. (Recipe collection of Sam Arnold.)

Tolling Antelope

Antelope meat tends to be both dry and very lean. Still, as the mountain men commonly said, "meat's meat, howsomever what kind, long as it's meat!" If the animal is young and well fed, it can be delicious.

From time to time on the prairie, Garrard and the others tolled antelope for a change of meat. Because these swift creatures are intensely curious and will investigate strange-looking activities, the practice of "tolling" was used. A tolling hunter would hide himself on the side of a hill. His assistant would appear at the top of another hill, standing on his head and shaking his legs in the air, sometimes with a large handkerchief tied to his ankles. Instead of running away, the fascinated antelope would approach within rifle range. Marcellus St. Vrain, brother of Ceran St. Vrain, was noted for his skill in tolling game.

*Meat Hunter
Waiting for the Wagons*

41

Skunk

In Major Long's expedition to the Rockies, and again in Lieutenant Abert's diary, there are references to eating skunk, or polecat. "[W]e found a polecat, *Mephitis americana*. The French people who were with us caught it and ate it. The odor, however, was too pungent to suit everyone's olfactories" (Abert, *Through the Country of the Comanche Indians*, 30).

Wild Birds and Fish by the Arkansas

On the Santa Fe Trail, Susan Magoffin noted, "we have fine grulla (sand cranes) today; they are tender and nice after being boiled nearly all night. The meat is black as pea fowls' " (Magoffin, 152). Bent's Fort hunters found a myriad of game fowl to put on the table. They hunted mourning doves, mallards, blue-wing teal, plovers, and killdeer. Catfish and hickory shad were the only Arkansas River fish reported by Lieutenant Abert.

References

Abert, Lieutenant James W. *Through the Country of the Comanche Indians in the Fall of the Year 1845*. Edited by John Galvin. San Francisco: John Howell Books, 1970.

[Abert, Lieutenant James W.] *Abert's New Mexico Report, 1846–47*. Albuquerque: Horn and Wallace, 1962.

Arnold, Sam. *Frying Pans West*. 11th ed. Denver: Arnold & Company, 1985.

Garrard, Lewis H. *Wah-To-Yah and the Taos Trail*. Norman: University of Oklahoma Press, 1955.

Gregg, Josiah. *Commerce of the Prairies*. Vol. 1. New York: Henry G. Langley, 1844. Reprint. Keystone Western Americana Series. Edited by Archibald Hanna and William H. Goetzmann. New York and Philadelphia: J. J. Lippincott Company, 1962.

The Journal of Captain John R. Bell, Official Journalist for the Stephen H. Long Expedition to the Rocky Mountains in 1820. Edited by Harlin M. Fuller and Leroy R. Hafen. Glendale, Calif.: Arthur H. Clark Company, 1957.

Lavender, David. *Bent's Fort*. Garden City, N.Y.: Doubleday & Co., 1954 (references to Fitzpatrick, 326; tolling antelope, 182; the hailstorm drink, 160).

Magoffin, Susan Shelby. *Down the Santa Fe Trail and Into Mexico: The Diary of Susan Shelby Magoffin, 1846–1847*. Edited by Stella M. Drumm. New Haven, Conn.: Yale University Press, 1926.

Stewart, William Drummund. *Edward Warren*. London: G. Walker, 1854. Reprint copyright Wilfred Blevins. Missoula, Mont.: Mountain Press Publishing Co., 1986.

Tucker, John M. "Major Long's Route From the Arkansas to the Canadian River, 1820." *New Mexico Historical Review*, Vol. 38, No. 3 (July 1963), 185–219.

Chapter 4

Contact with the Indians

Cheyenne Woman in summer calioe
based on Tracy Johnson

Leaving Westport in the company of a wagon train, many a pilgrim looked forward with curiosity, and some fear, to seeing western Indians. During the earlier days of the trail, there had been some serious attacks on travelers, but as time passed, the wagon trains grew stronger and Indian attacks grew fewer, though they still posed a serious problem. In response to this threat, the military set up forts along the route beginning in the 1850s to protect both the wagon trains and the settlers who chose to live in the new territories.

Indian Enemies

Besides hunting, the male Plains Indian's lifework was war, which he waged against hereditary enemies. It was Crow against Sioux; Southern Cheyenne and Arapahoe against Pawnee; Navajo and Apache against Pueblo. Mountain men who trapped beaver often lived in Indian villages that were friendly to them. Although the Indians' enemies became their enemies, the way of life in such a village also had its pleasures; the Indians soon saw that at the annual trading get-together called "rendezvous" and at the forts, one could trade for all manner of exciting new joys.

Diluted or Doped Alcohol

Of all the desired items in the western Indian trade, alcohol was number one in importance. Fur traders found early on that they could successfully sell highly diluted alcohol to the Indians. By cutting it to less than 5 percent, the traders were able to amass large profits per gallon — as much as 10,000 percent. With the alcohol cut so thin, they would often add other items for taste. The recipe for Injun Whiskey in Chapter 2, for example, calls for red pepper, tobacco juice, and black gunpowder, a surprisingly tasty combination. It was said that in later years, when good pure whiskey came into Indian country, it was rejected because it "didn't have that good old-fashioned flavor."

In his book *Rocky Mountain Life*, Rufus B. Sage reported that in 1842, at Fort Laramie in eastern Wyoming, the American Fur Company carried on doping of alcohol with laudanum. It was the fur company's belief that spiking the alcohol with an opium tincture would slow down the violence that often followed big Indian drinking parties. A number of Indians died from overdoses. Sage's description follows:

> Men, women, and children were seen running from lodge to lodge with vessels of liquor, inviting their friends and relatives to drink; while whooping, singing, drunkenness, and trading for fresh supplies to administer to the demands of intoxication, had evidently become the order of the day. Soon, individuals were noticed passing from one to another, with mouths full of the coveted firewater, drawing the lips of their favored friends in close contact, as if to kiss, and ejecting the contents of their own into the eager mouths of the others — thus affording the delighted recipients tastes of their fervent esteem in the heat and strength of the strange draught (Sage, 100–101).

With the serious Indian behavior problems frequently faced by traders Sage wrote that

> the American Fur Company . . . commenced dealing out . . . gratuitously, strong drugged liquor, for the double purpose of preventing a sale of the article by its competitor in trade, and of creating sickness, or inciting contention among the Indians, while under the influence of sudden intoxication — hoping thereby to induce the latter to charge its ill effects upon an opposite source, and thus, by destroying the credit of its rival, monopolize for itself the whole trade.
>
> . . . Already its effects became apparent, and small knots of drunken Indians were seen in various directions, quarreling, preparing to fight, or fighting — while others lay stretched upon the ground in helpless impotency, or staggered from place to place with all of the revolting attendancies of intoxication (Sage, 101).

Indian Trading

After many visits from the chiefs asking for liquor, traders began trading away from the fort two or three times a year. George Grinnell describes a liquor-trading visit to an Indian camp:

> A trader coming into the village deposited the [liquor] kegs, of various sizes, at the lodge of a chief. The Indians then came to the lodge and offered what they had to trade, and each man was assigned a keg of a certain size, according to the number of robes or the horses or mules he had offered to trade. Each Indian then tied to his keg a piece of cloth or a string to mark it as his, and it was left in the chief's lodge, unopened, for the present. When the trade had been completed the trader left the village, and not until he had gone some distance did the chief permit the Indians to take their kegs of liquor and open them.... No trader wanted whiskey in the camp where he was working. The presence of liquor in the camp not only ended all trade, but often endangered the trader's life.
>
> Nearly all of the whiskey that reached the Indians in the country south of the Platte came from New Mexico. The Mexicans peddled the liquor among the Indians themselves when they dared, but when this was too dangerous, they sold the stuff to lawless Americans who took it to the Indian camps (Grinnell, 32).

In 1835, Colonel Henry Dodge, leader of a group of dragoons who visited Bent's Fort in that year, found Mexicans from Taos on the Mexican side of the Arkansas River engaged in selling liquor to the Cheyennes. John C. Fremont, who was known as "the Pathfinder" and made four western expeditions to locate prospective railroad routes to California, later stated that a small keg of this liquor was traded to the Indians for the equivalent of $36 in goods (this at a time when one could hire a man's services for $7 per month).

Dog Stew

Perhaps the best-loved dish among most Plains Indians was dog stew. A young pup of 6 to 8 weeks, preferably still milk fed, would be seized by its hind legs by the cook, who would dispatch it with a sharp rap of its head on a rock. After skinning and eviscerating, the carcass was cut up into pieces and thrown in the pot with wild onions, prairie potatoes, and sufficient water. There was rarely any salt, and Indians were not accustomed to eating salted foods. If the cook was fortunate enough to have a metal pot or dutch oven, the stew was cooked in this. Later variations included the addition of ordinary onions, carrots and potatoes, ingredients brought by white settlers.

One western traveler named J. Henry Carleton noted:

> If a Pawnee honours you with a feast, you must expect to be regaled on dog meat as a matter of course, besides you must eat out of the same ladle with all the other guests — taking a mouthful of meat and a drink of broth, and then passing it around on the same principle as the pipe. Dog soup is the favorite dish of the Pawnees, Sioux, Crows, Blackfeet, and Cheyennes (Irving, *Indian Sketches*, 197).

In his book *Wah-To-Yah and the Taos Trail*, Lewis Garrard described being tricked by Uncle John Smith, a traveling companion and famed mountain man, into eating dog stew. He wrote:

> It was now quite late, and feeling hungry, I asked what was on the fire?
>
> "Tarrapins!" promptly replied Smith.
>
> "Terrapins?" echoed I, in surprise, at the name. "Terrapins! how do they cook them?"
>
> "You know them hard-shell land tarrapin?"
>
> "Yes."
>
> "Well! the squaws go out to the sand buttes, and bring the critters in, and cook 'em in the shell alive — those stewin' thar ar [sic] cleaned first. Howsomever, they're darned good!"
>
> "Yes, Hos, an' that's a fact, wagh!" chimed in Greenwood [another of Garrard's traveling companions].
>
> I listened, of course, with much interest to their account of the savage dish, and waited, with impatience for a taste of that, the recital of whose merits sharpened my already keen appetite. When the squaw transferred the contents of the kettle to wooden bowl and passed it to us, our butcher knives were in immediate requisition.

Taking a piece, with hungry avidity, which Smith handed me, without thought as to what part of the terrapin it was, I ate it with much gusto, calling "for more." It was extremely good, and I spoke of the delicacy of the meat, and answered all their questions as to its excellency in the affirmative, even to the extent of a panegyric on the whole turtle species. After fully committing myself, Smith looked at me awhile in silence, the corners of his mouth gradually making preparations for a laugh, and asked:

"Well, hos! how do you like dogmeat?" and then such hearty guffaws were never heard. The stupefaction into which I was thrown by the revolting announcement only increased their merriment, which soon was resolved into yells of delight at my discomfiture. A revulsion of opinion, and dogmeat too, ensued, for I could feel the "pup" crawling up my throat. But, saying to myself "that it was good under the name of terrapin," "that a rose under any other name would smell as sweet," and that it would be prejudice to stop, I broke the shackles of deep-rooted antipathy to the canine breed, and, putting a choice [*morceau*] on top of that already swallowed, ever after remained a staunch defender and admirer of dogmeat (Garrard, 78–79).

Garrard goes on to describe an Indian method for preparing dog stew:

Se-ne-mone's squaw gave a dogfeast one day. As the Indians are great epicures, the modus operandi of preparation may not be uninteresting to our more civilized gourmands, whose tables are bare of a viand, which, undoubtedly, ranks preeminent in the list of delicacies and luxuries.

First, a pup of four months' sojourn in this world of sorrow, so fat he could scarcely waddle, was caught by the affectionate squaw, and turned, and felt, and pinched, to see whether it would do. Then its neck was invested with one end of a buckskin strap, and the other tied short up to the projecting coupling pole of our wagon, while the poor victim to savage appetite, dangling between earth and sky, ki-ed until his little canine spirit departed for the elysium where neither squaws molest nor dogmeat is eaten, to the very apparent satisfaction of the laughing women, and delighted children, and the no small annoyance of many large dogs, among whom was the disconsolate mother of the unfortunate. She sent forth, with head and neck elongated, most piteous bewailings, until receiving a kick from one of the amazons, which sent her off limping, filling the air with discordant

Indian Woman in her finery

yells, fully as painful to us as was the kick to the recipient of the squaw's marked attentions. She sat on her haunches, at a little distance from us, now and then raising her paw — not to brush away the falling tear, but to rub her nose, on which had fallen the cruel blow.

After hanging half an hour, the pup was taken down and laid on the fire. What! thought I, they are not so heathenish as to offer sacrifices? He was kept on the blaze, with constant turning, until the hair was well singed off, and then cleaned, beheaded, and divided into all imaginable shapes and sizes, and cooked in water for six hours. It was then fished out, and a portion set before us — a slimy, glutinous mass, uninviting to the eye, but, nevertheless, most delicate and sweet. Smith laid by one of the hind legs until the next morning; the marbled thin streaks of lean and fat, were most tempting. It reminded me of cold roast pig — a faint simile, probably derogatory to the fair fame of "dog" and for which degenerate, civilized comparison, I humbly crave the pardon of Se-ne-mone's spouse, and her worthy curs (Garrard, 93–95).

Another Cheyenne dish Garrard mentions is "dried stewed pumpkin with a horned spoon sticking in it by which we partook by turns" (Garrard, 61). Cheyennes purchased food from small parties of New Mexicans who came from Taos Valley trading dried pumpkin, corn, and pinole for buffalo robes and meat.

Pemmican

These days, backpackers and mountain climbers are familiar with pemmican, possibly the most widely eaten traditional Indian food. At the time of the Santa Fe Trail, it was called the "iron ration" of the Indian warrior. Mountain men and Indian alike enjoyed the combination of chokecherries mixed with well-pounded dry jerky and a nearly equal amount of rendered tallow fat (the purest fat surrounds an animal's kidneys). Pemmican was normally formed by hand into small walnut-sized balls and could be stored individually. It could also be forced into an empty bladder, where it would keep for long periods.

Indian Delicacies

When scraping down the hide of a buffalo, the squaws used a sharp, adz-shaped tool to chip off small hide shavings. These shavings were carefully collected until enough were available for a "nice feast." The chips were put in a wooden bowl and covered with boiling water, which cooked and reduced the shavings to a pulpy mass that tasted similar to boiled Irish potatoes (Garrard, 119). Chokecherries were added for a "fancy flavor." The Cheyenne women also gathered the fungus growing on the sides of decaying logs and boiled it with meat for several hours. The resulting dish tasted like fine oysters. Garrard also mentions that a "root growing in the bottoms is much eaten, raw or cooked, partaking both of the flavor of the potato and Jerusalem artichoke" (Garrard, 67).

Paunch Cooking

Before the advent of traders with metal kettles, Plains Indians used the paunch of the buffalo or other animal as a cooking pot for meat and broth. The large stomach was removed during butchering, emptied of grass, washed clean, and set aside to serve as the cooking kettle. Four sturdy forked sticks were driven into the ground in a square, and the paunch was suspended between them. The paunch was then filled with water and freshly cut pieces of meat.

Nearby, a roaring fire heated round, smooth, stream-bed rocks until they were cherry-red. A forked stick in one hand and poker in the other were used to convey hot rocks to the paunch, into which the rocks were dropped, hissing when they hit the water. After about the seventh rock, the water began to boil furiously. When the heat subsided, the cooling rocks were fished out and new hot ones added, keeping the mass boiling for several hours. The remaining rocks were then removed and the meat and broth eaten. When the contents were gone, the paunch itself was cut up and eaten.

Having shared a paunch with a Rosebud Sioux family, I find that the bland odor and mild taste of supermarket beef bears no relation to the basic, earthy, manure odors and flavors found in freshly field-killed Rosebud Indian beef cut up with a Green River knife and cooked in a paunch! Chewing the paunch meat itself is rather like chewing on a tough car inner tube.

Soups or stews made from broth of jerked meat, prairie onions, dried corn, and diced wild turnips were common.

Blue Corn

Among the Plains Indians, sunflower seeds were often ground for meal and used as a tasty thickening for stews.

Wo-ja-pi

A Plains Indian dish still enjoyed today by the old people at feasts and dances is wo-ja-pi (pronounced whoa-zha-pee). Ripe chokecherries are picked in early fall and mashed together, seeds and all. Small cakes are formed and allowed to dry. When ready to use them, the Indians soak the cakes in water until they are soft, then pulverize them with a stone mallet. The pulverized dried chokecherries are then cooked in a kettle of water with flour and sugar to form a cooked, sweet, thin, fruity paste that is very good cold. The bits of broken seed are hard on the teeth. Stewed dried sumac berries may also be cooked as a version of wo-ja-pi.

Recipe for Wo-ja-pi

Grind berries with mortar and pestle, or with a rock mallet in a large rawhide bowl. Place berries in a pot with water. Add flour and stir mixture to boiling. Add sugar and cook till thickened. (I watched an old Rosebud Sioux lady make this dish in South Dakota in 1969 while filming my TV show "Frying Pans West.")

1 quart dried chokecherries
  or sumac berries
3 quarts water
¾ cup sugar
5 tablespoons ordinary flour

To make White Man's Wo-ja-pi, cook blackberries, boysenberries, or, if you can gather them when ripe and sweet in the fall, wild chokecherries. Try to remove the large, ball-shaped seeds with a food mill or a fine sieve. I have successfully removed chokecherry seeds from pulp by using a food processor with a plastic dough-mixer blade, using rapid on-off switching. Cook this fruit pulp with water, two cups of sugar, and two tablespoons ordinary flour mixed into water. Grate peel from one-half lemon into the mix and boil slowly until flour is cooked (about 15 minutes). Chill and serve. Some whipped cream or ice cream on top is a great addition, though not historically accurate. (Recipe collection of Sam Arnold.)

Was-nah is a Sioux Indian name for a sweetened toasted-corn dessert. Here is a recipe from Loves Horses, a Lakota Sioux lady who lived with my family in 1963:

Was-nah

2 cups toasted cornmeal
½ pound butter or rendered beef kidney-fat oil
2 cups brown sugar
2 cups pitted cherries, canned or fresh, or ripe chokecherries

Spread cornmeal on a cookie sheet and toast it in the oven, being careful not to let it burn. Stir cornmeal around so that it toasts to an even, golden brown. Mix all ingredients and allow to cool in refrigerator. When solidified, give each person about one tablespoonful molded into a ball. It is sweet and nourishing and makes a great snack for children. The toasted cornmeal has something of the flavor of popcorn, and with the butter, sugar, and cherries, it is simply delicious. To make the dish more authentically Indian, replace the butter with kidney fat from a buffalo or beef and grind it fine, rendering out the oil over a low heat.

In *Rocky Mountain Life*, Rufus Sage wrote on Christmas Day, 1841:

Several little extras for the occasion have been procured from the Indians, which prove quite wholesome and pleasant-tasted. One of these, called washena [was-nah], consists of dried meat, pulverized and mixed with marrow; another is a preparation of cherries, preserved when first picked, by pounding and sun-drying them (they are served by mixing them with bouillie, or the liquor of fresh-boiled meat, thus giving to it an agreeable winish taste); a third is marrow-fat, an article in many respects superior to butter; and, lastly, we obtained a kind of flour made from the pomme blanc (white apple), answering very well as a substitute for that of grain (Sage, 112).

Quail

Wash-tunk-ala

This is the name for a dried deer or buffalo meat and corn stew favored by the Sioux and other Plains Indians.

Mix all ingredients except cornmeal to make a soup. Add a little cold water to cornmeal, mix, then add to soup. Simmer for 2 hours. Skim and serve. (I also learned this recipe from Loves Horses.)

2 pounds jerked meat (beef, buffalo, deer, or elk) cut in bite-sized pieces

2 quarts water

24 reconstituted prairie potatoes or 4 large, red potatoes, peeled and cut into bite-sized pieces

3 ears dried corn reconstituted by overnight soaking, cut into discs, or one fresh ear in 1-inch discs

2 commotes, a type of wild tuber (carrots cut in pieces may be substituted)

6 wild onions, cut diagonally in one-inch pieces (green onions or scallions may be substituted)

1 large red pepper cut into bite-sized pieces

3 tablespoons cornmeal

salt and black pepper to taste (red chiles may be substituted)

There are certainly other versions of Wash-tunk-ala. Because pepper was unknown and very little salt was available, Wash-tunk-ala and similar stews provided only the basic flavor of the ingredients. The stew tastes somewhat bland to today's palate and benefits from the addition of salt and black pepper. Indians without salt sometimes roasted coltsfoot stalks to provide a salt substitute.

Prairie Potatoes and Commote

Prairie potatoes (*Psoralea esculenta*) are often found on hillsides, and when the plant was identified, the Indian dug it up, extracting the tuber's bulb. The bulb was washed, stripped clean of its black skin, and strung to dry like garlic. An overnight soaking reconstituted this pithy potato substitute that tastes slightly like turnip.

The prairie potato, or *pomme blanche* (white apple), is a native of the prairie and mountains. Oval shaped and about 3-½ inches in circumference, it is encased in a thin, fibrous skin, which, when removed, exposes white pulpy material like a turnip in taste. It generally grows at a depth of 3 to 4 inches in the soil of hillsides and plateaus where a reddish clay loam is found. The stalk attains a height of about 3 inches and looks like sheep sorrel. Its white flowers blossom in late spring.

The *commote*, another edible root found in the West, is much like the ordinary radish in size and shape. It has a brown skin covering a soft, milky-white inside that is both flavorful and nutritious. It is most often found in river bottoms and requires a rich, loamy, vegetable-mat soil. It grows about 4 inches deep, and its leaves resemble a carrot's in shape and color. The commote rarely grows more than 2 inches above the ground and has a pretty blue blossom. Both the pomme blanche and commote are equally good raw or boiled.

Fry Bread

Traditional fry bread is delicious when eaten as it comes from the fat. It has become so much a part of Plains Indian life that Native Americans today often believe it is part of their long heritage. However, fried foods were unknown to the Indians until metal kettles were introduced by the white man. Attend any powwow, big dinner, or Indian event, and you'll find fry bread. It's one "white-eyes" food that has become part of Indian life (wheat flour is another).

Plains Indian fried bread is very much the same as Pueblo or Navajo fried bread — a yeast or baking-powder bread dough rolled out and cut into squares or shaped into rounds, then fried until puffed up and browned all over (spooning hot fat over the bread while frying makes it puff up).

Squaw Bread (Fried Bread)

4 cups flour
4 teaspoons baking powder
2 teaspoons salt
2 heaping teaspoons sugar
1-⅓ cups water

Mix dry ingredients well and add about one and one-third cups lukewarm water to make dough. Roll out, cut into rectangles, and fry in deep fat. (Recipe collection of Sam Arnold.)

Cornmeal and sunflower-seed meal were important staples of the Indian diet. In some tribal areas where oak trees were found (in the Dakotas, Colorado, and most often reported in California), acorns were also used for meal. They were gathered, ground, and washed with boiling water poured through a sieve to leach out the poisonous tannic acid. The meal was then dried and used for making cakes or mush.

California Indians prepared a cold biscuit by mixing water with a considerable amount of previously leached acorn meal

EATING UP THE SANTA FE TRAIL

and cooking it until almost stiff. Small muffin-shaped baskets served as molds. The baskets, filled with meal mush, were put in water and when they were quite cold, a few taps would loosen the gelatinous biscuit from the basket. It had to be quite cold in order to set. Acorn meal was also flavored with fresh berries or clover pulp. Acorn cakes were baked on hot stones or dried on rocks under the sun.

Piñon Nuts

In scrub-pine areas, piñon nuts were used for making a thick soup. Meat and pine nuts were added to chopped onion and dried mint leaves in a soup. More about piñon nuts in Chapter 8.

Innards

The heart, liver, and kidneys of game were considered choice parts by the Plains Indian. Upon killing a deer or buffalo, the Indian would clean the animal, recovering the fresh kidneys and liver. Often the gallbladder was removed intact and pricked. The green gall juice was then sprinkled over cuts of liver or raw kidney, "by way of zest" according to Sage in *Rocky Mountain Life*. He extols the beneficial nature of buffalo gall as a cure-all for dyspepsia and any other ulcerous condition of the stomach:

> It is prepared . . . with one pint of water mix[ed] with one-fourth gill of buffalo-gall . . . a wholesome and exhilerating [sic] drink. To a stomach unaccustomed to its use it may at first create a slightly noisome sensation, like the inceptive effects of an emetic; and, to one strongly bilious, it might cause vomiting; but on the second or third trial, the stomach attains a taste for it, and receives it with no inconsiderable relief. Upon the whole system its effects are beneficial. As a stimulant, it braces the nerves without producing a corresponding relaxation on the cessation of its influence; it also tends to restore an impaired appetite and invigorate the digestive powers. As a sanative [sic], it tends to make sound an irritated and ulcerated stomach, reclaiming it to a healthy and lively tone, and thus striking an effective blow at that most prolific source of so large a majority of the diseases common to civil[i]zed life.
>
> . . . I consider it one of the most innocent and useful medicines in cases of dyspepsy, and will hazard the further

opinion, that, were those laboring under the wasting influences of this disease to drink "gall-bitters," thousands who are now pining away by piecemeal, would be restored to perfect soundness and snatched from the very threshold from a certain grave which yawns to receive them (Sage, 178–179).

Chokecherry Tea

Traveler Rufus Sage also described a tea made from wild cherry bark — probably the same tea used some years earlier to cure Merriwether Lewis on the Lewis and Clark expedition. Wild cherry bark (from chokecherry bushes) was boiled to make a tea that was popular among mountaineers and Indians, who drank it during the spring season, believing it useful "for purifying the blood and reducing it to suitable consistency for the temperature of summer" (Sage, 147). Chokecherry bark tea was most commonly used as a remedy for diarrhea. Chokecherries (*Prunus virginiana*) grow over much of America. Another wild cherry known as pincherry (*Prunus pennsylvanica*) and a bush cherry (*Prunus bessevi*) grow in the Rocky Mountain area. Both provide edible fruit.

Dried stewed sumac berries were used by Indians and mountain men in much of the West. Both the green and the ripe berries were eaten either raw or cooked. The berries were made into sun-dried cakes similar to dried chokecherry cakes. These cakes were often dried and stored for the winter. Having a sharp acidic flavor, the berries were also used to make a drink similar to our lemonade.

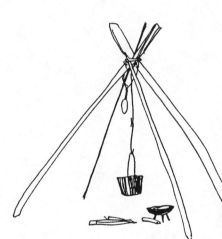

Kinnikinnik

In *Through the Country of the Comanche Indians*, Lieutenant Abert, camped on the north fork of the Canadian River, reported great quantities of sumac. "[T]his is much used by the Comanches in making their kinnikinnik which they prepare by wilting the leaves over a moderate fire. The Shawnees and other tribes about Westport use the inner bark of the willow while the tribes on the border of the Great Lakes use the wintergreen and bark of the maple; in fact, almost every tribe uses a different plant" (Abert, 59).

Kinnikinnik is an Algonquin Indian word meaning roughly "that which is mixed together for smoking." In its original meaning, it is not a specific plant or formula. Many barks, roots, and leaves were used for making various smoking mixtures, and any combination could be termed kinnikinnik.

The most common combination used by Plains Indians is one-third bearberry plant leaves (known in the Rocky Mountains as kinnikinnik), one-third inside bark of red osier (the switch-like red willow that grows along streams), and one-third cut plug Kentucky burley tobacco. Squaw and skunk sumac leaves were also used (Abert, 59). (I have made excellent kinnikinnik by picking bearberry plant leaves in Colorado late in the season. They are dried and lightly roasted for five minutes on a cookie sheet in a 350° F. oven. When combined with equal amounts of tobacco and red osier, this mixture seems to have a sedative effect.)

Indian Cooking Tools

A tool found universally among the Indians was the mortar. It served as a base on which to grind everything from corn and seeds to berries. To make one, a hollow was formed in a block of wood by repeatedly kindling a fire on top of the block and scraping out the burned wood until the resulting hollow was as large as needed. The mortar was generally 1 foot in diameter and about 8 inches deep. The pestle was formed from a knobby piece of hard wood. Each family had its own mortar and pestle, which the squaws would bring to a common area near the fire. Corn-grinding time was also a social hour.

Indian Dining Protocol

In his book *Indian Sketches*, written during an expedition to the Pawnee tribes in 1833, John Treat Irving, Jr., describes the protocol of a meal:

> When we had seated ourselves, a large bowl of boiled buffalo flesh was placed before us, and signs made for us to fall to. The chief himself acted as master of ceremonies. He thrust his hands into the bowl, and turned over and over the heap of smoking meat, selecting the best morsel (for us), and welcoming us. . . . [W]ith all his jovial appearance, there was a cowering look about his eye, when he met the vinegar glance of one or two of his oldest wives. . . . It is customary for the guest, when he is unable to dispose of the whole provision placed before him, to send what is left to his own

quarters. The duty of carrying it is generally entrusted to one of the junior members of the family who, when departing upon his errand, receives a particular caution from the squaw to be careful and bring back the bowl (Irving, 163–164).

Irving also described the spearing of a "sodden and water-soaked boiled pumpkin" from a large kettle hanging over the fire. "How we managed to get through that vegetable feast I can hardly say. It was one of the severest trials of the whole of our campaign; yet we did get through with it and emerged from the lodge in safety" (Irving, 165).

A Repulsive Meal

Indian standards of food sanitation rarely pleased touring easterners or Europeans. In a visit to the Otoe Indians, who lived in Kansas and Oklahoma, Prince Paul of Wurttemberg is quoted in Irving's *Indian Sketches* as follows:

> We had to accompany the first chief into his hut where the ceremonies prescribed by the Indian code of civility took place . . . a most repulsive meal which was prepared in my honor. It consisted of dog meat and jerked dried buffalo meat. This tempting meal was boiled with corn. The kettle in which the ingredients were contained was badly in need of scouring. The scum was being skimmed off with a most unappetizing horn spoon. I left the hut for a few minutes. Mr. Riley, however, called me back and said that the Indians would be very much offended if I should disdain their meal. He said I should control myself and at least pretend to partake of it. I therefore returned, but was again seized with revulsion when an old dirty woman picked up the meat out of the kettle with her dirty hands, and greedily sipped the meat broth out of her hollowed hands. I exerted all my will-power to suppress the terrible repugnance I felt, but could not force myself to swallow an entire spoonful of the food. . . . When I sipped of it, the Indians were content (Irving, p. 81f, n. 3).

Some of the even less-appetizing-sounding Indian dishes included dried buffalo lung; buffalo blood congealed with stomach rennet into a jelly; bison and moose nose; upper intestines filled with grasses, tied off and set in the sun to ferment; and prairie dog droppings and red ant cakes (often a staple of the Diggers or Paiutes). While these may sound unappetizing, reserve judgment until you taste them.

References

Abert, Lieutenant James W. *Through the Country of the Comanche Indians in the Fall of the Year 1845*. Edited by John Galvin. San Francisco: John Howell Books, 1970.

Arnold, Sam. *Frying Pans West*. 11th ed. Denver: Arnold & Company, 1985.

Frazer, Robert W. *Forts of the West*. Norman: University of Oklahoma Press, 1972.

Fremont, Brevet Capt. J. C. *Narrative of the Exploring Expedition to the Rocky Mountains in the Year 1842, and to Oregon and North California in the Years 1843–44*. Syracuse, N.Y.: A. L. Smith, 1846.

Garrard, Lewis H. *Wah-To-Yah and the Taos Trail*. Norman: University of Oklahoma Press, 1955.

Grinnell, George Bird. *Bent's Old Fort and Its Builders*. Wichita: Kansas Historical Society, 1912.

Irving, John Treat, Jr. *Indian Sketches*. Edited by J. F. McDermott. Norman: University of Oklahoma Press, 1955.

Lavender, David. *Bent's Fort*. Garden City, N.Y.: Doubleday & Co., 1954 (references to Colonel Dodge, 160).

Linsenmeyer, Helen Walker. *From Fingers to Finger Bowls*. San Diego: Copley Books, 1976 (reference to acorn meal, 6–8).

Sage, Rufus B. *Rocky Mountain Life, or Startling Scenes and Perilous Adventure, in the Far West*. Dayton, Ohio: Edward Canby, 1846.

Chapter 5

Military Forts on the Trail

From the early days of the Santa Fe Trail, Indians had looked upon the intruding travelers as a source of treasure, which sometimes came to them in gifts, sometimes in trade, but most often by theft and violence. Among the raiding tribes were the Kaw (and other Sioux) and Pawnees in Kansas; the Kiowas and Comanches; and, further west, the Cheyenne, Arapahoe, Apaches, Navajo, and Utes. Hostilities were frequent. Settlers didn't appreciate the threats and murders; the Native Americans didn't like the white invaders.

The federal government responded to the frontier violence by erecting lines of forts along the trails. These forts were designed primarily to protect local settlers, commercial freighters, and settler wagon trains from Indian raids. In later years, these military bases also served to protect the reservation Indians from white depredations, to keep peace and order, and to prevent white settlers from encroaching on Indian treaty land.

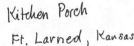

Kitchen Porch
Ft. Larned, Kansas

In 1851, there were more than 1,300 troopers stationed along the westward trails in the Territory of New Mexico alone. Seeking to counteract the "temptations" of wine, gambling, and women in Santa Fe, the military transferred much of the personnel of Fort Marcy to newly built Fort Union, out in desolate country, several days journey northeast of Santa Fe.

Shortly after the Santa Fe Trail opened in 1821, politicians and entrepreneurs called for military convoys to escort the freight wagon trains to Santa Fe. Senator Thomas Hart Benton exerted so much political pressure that a road was finally surveyed in the mid-1820s and military personnel assigned to various forts to protect commerce. Major Bennett Riley took four companies of infantry down the trail in 1829, only to find that infantry was virtually useless against mounted Indians. From that time on, the Dragoons and the Mounted Rifles, the forerunners of the U.S. Cavalry, became the "guardians of the West."

At the eastern end of the trail, Fort Osage was built in 1808 on the Missouri River near Leavenworth, Kansas, as a trade fort. A fortified trading house, or factory, as these government-sponsored trade centers were called, provided Kansas and Osage Indians with trade goods such as beads, tobacco, cloth, blankets, and axe heads in exchange for furs. Foodstuffs such as bacon, salt pork, and wheat flour were also traded. In 1823, two years after the Santa Fe Trail opened, Fort Osage was abandoned.

In 1829, Major Bennett Riley left Fort Leavenworth, in Kansas, to protect an eastbound freight wagon train coming from New Mexico. At Chouteau's Island in the Arkansas River, which then formed the U.S.-Mexican border, Riley met the train, which had been accompanied to that point by a Mexican Army escort. Riley's men, the Mexican soldiers, and the members of the wagon train had a meal together, described by one of Riley's officers:

> Seated cross-legged around a green blanket in the bottom of the tent, we partook of bread, buffalo meat, and as an extraordinary rarity, of some salt pork, but to crown all were several large onions for which we were indebted to our arriving guests. A tin cup of whiskey, which, like the pork, had been reserved for an unusual occasion, was followed by another of water (Cooke, *Scenes and Adventures in the Army*, 85–87).

Supplying the forts of the West became Fort Leavenworth's primary duty, and General William Tecumseh Sherman, a former Leavenworth lawyer, summed up its role, calling it "the most valuable military reservation in the west." Its Command and General Staff College remains one of the world's top schools for military instruction.

At the western forts, men of each company commonly ate together at mealtime. They sat on bench seats at long, bare, wooden tables and ate from a tin plate and drank from a large tin cup. Senior non-commissioned personnel often ate at separate, smaller tables in a gentlemanly effort, often bringing their own tablecloths, napkins, and even monogrammed silverware. New recruits were hazed, or unmercifully teased. At one post, new recruits were seriously told that the local "hog ranch" was their source of pork. Another man was a source of hilarity when, having been ordered to split a huge quantity of peas for split pea soup, he tried vainly to do his duty with a paring knife.

Out in the field, soldiers carried rations of coffee, hardtack, sugar, and salt pork. Each man usually carried his own food for at least one day. In Don Rickey's book *Forty Miles a Day on Beans and Hay,* he describes the miseries of men carrying salt pork in their meat ration cans. In the hot sun, the pork fat melted and ran out of the cans. Hardtack in haversacks broke up, crumbling, and making a mess. Each man had his own water canteen, and, hopefully, there was a water wagon included in the column. One soldier described the monotony of the field diet: "We now have a change of diet, Hardtack, bacon and coffee for breakfast; raw bacon and tack for dinner; fried bacon and hard bread for supper" (Rickey, *Forty Miles a Day on Beans and Hay,* 248). "The tack had bugs in it, and the bacon had worms too . . . anything was good enough for a soldier," noted another member of the military (Rickey, 248–249).

Salt pork was first parboiled, then impaled on a stick and placed to broil over the fire. It could also be fried in the mess kit or in a light frying pan. Some dipped it in vinegar and ate it raw. Hardtack, when dampened, fried in salt pork drippings, and sprinkled with brown sugar, made a make-shift dessert. Pulverized hardtack, bacon, and raisins, boiled in condensed milk, was cooked up by Trumpeter Mulford and his Seventh Cavalry "bunkie" in 1877 (Rickey, 249).

From a camp near Ft. Larned on April 9, 1867, one soldier wrote his wife:

What do you think I had for dinner? Why, a big plumb [sic] pudding! Fact! . . . and soft bread and butter and meat (boiled tongue and ham) and "hard tack," and baked beans (I have a bake kettle and "Dutch Oven") and coffee, canned peaches; and cooked out in the "big field" and in the driving snow. I have an excellent cook, but how he manages to get along today is more than I can see. We have a little mess chest exactly like Lt. Wallingford's, white plates, cups and saucers, glass drinking goblets, etc. We still have about 10 pounds of butter left. General Custer has a barrel of apples along. We are now in the midst of a great buffalo range. Thousands upon thousands of them are said to be just south of us. The head of a buffalo which was killed a week or two ago lies outside my tent. It is a monstrous sight, twice as large as the head of an ox, and there is matted hair (almost wool) enough on it to stuff a buggy cushion. The mouth and nose are very small, not larger than those of a yearling calf (Personal correspondence of a soldier from Fort Larned to his wife).

In 1863, at Fort Larned's store, there were many varieties of canned goods, including tomatoes, peaches, and strawberries. Perhaps strangest of all were the cans of lobster meat — priced at $.50 each! Beer cost $1 a gallon, whiskey $1.50 a gallon; tea was quite expensive at $1.25 per pound.

The following recipes for Hardcrackers and Army Bread come from Fort Larned National Historical Site in western Kansas.

Hardcrackers, or Hard Tack

Knead flour, water, and salt; roll out on greased 12-by-13-inch pan; cut into fifteen pieces; pierce each piece with sixteen holes. Bake for 30 minutes at 425º F., 15 minutes on each side. Reduce temperature to 200º F. and bake until all moisture is removed from crackers (approximately 8 to 24 hours. Crackers will not burn in a 200º F. oven, so may remain in oven almost indefinitely.)

4 to 5 cups flour
2 cups water
2 pinches salt

Army Bread

Stir thoroughly, adding flour gradually until the dough is too thick to stir with a spoon. Turn out on a floured table and knead until smooth and elastic. Place in a greased bowl and let rise. When double in bulk, punch down and let dough rise again. When doubled in bulk, divide dough into six or eight equal portions and put in pans. Let rise again until nearly double in size, place in pre-heated oven, and bake

1 package yeast
2 cups lukewarm water
2 cups flour
Mix above ingredients, stir, and let sit at room temperature overnight. In the morning, add
4 cups lukewarm water
6 teaspoons salt
flour

until done. Suggested temperature is 375º F. for 40 to 45 minutes for single loaves or 1 hour or more for multiloaf pans.

The sameness of rations encouraged innovation, and a living off the land. For many soldiers in the field, jackrabbits, wild birds and fish, deer and antelope, and the occasional buffalo provided variety in field foodstuffs. Back at the forts, there was traditionally a sutler's store, where all manner of food and drink might be bought. The Bent, St. Vrain & Company's freighters, among others, brought wide varieties of foods. Spruce beer, sardines, oysters, and even caviar were available. Since the army didn't pay its enlisted men well, most of the highly priced foods were bought by the officers and their wives.

Fresh and dried apples were basic staples for the forts. But sometimes, the fruit simply didn't arrive in the freight wagons. Ingenious settlers developed a recipe for apple pie without apples, to be used during these dire emergencies. Here's the recipe. Remarkably, it tastes just like apple pie!

Apple Pie Without Apples, or Mock Apple Pie

2 cups soda crackers
2 eggs
1 cup sugar or ½ cup honey
1 cup milk
1 teaspoon nutmeg
2 teaspoons cinnamon
½ lemon rind, grated
double-crust pie shell
2 tablespoons butter

Beat eggs and mix with soda crackers, sugar, milk, and spices. Fill pie shell. Grate lemon peel on top of filling and spread. Dot with butter. Cover with top crust, forking a few vents in the crust. Bake 40 minutes at 325º F. (I found this recipe at Fort Robinson, Nebraska. It was called Mock Apple Pie. A variation of this recipe was published in the 1930s by the Ritz Cracker Company, and for some years it was again a popular dessert.)

In later years, there were many military installations along the Santa Fe Trail: Fort Riley, near Junction City; Fort Zarah, by Great Bend and Walnut Creek; Fort Larned, just west of Pawnee Fork; Fort Mann, later renamed Fort Atkinson; and Fort Dodge, all in Kansas. These forts guarded roads in the Santa Fe Trail trade. One of the few comforts issued to the men was a ration of rum. In 1850, coffee replaced the rum, to nearly everyone's disgust. Government-issued green coffee was roasted in a frying pan, put in a sock or bag, and beaten to a powder by gun butt.

After General Kearny's Army of the West came down the trail in the summer of 1846, there was a long littered trail of empty sardine cans left behind (sardines were easy to carry). General Kearny had made provision for meat in part by sending herds of cattle ahead to be consumed along the way. But "Old Ned," as they called salt pork, was the army's mainstay.

Salt Pork with Mashed Peas for One Hundred Men

Wrap the meat and peas in four pudding-cloth bags. Boil meat and peas in two pots for 4 hours. After 2 hours, remove the bags and put all the meat in one pot. Remove the liquor from the other pot and put the peas back into it. Add pepper and one pound of the fat [a piece of the salt pork] to the peas, and with a wooden spatula, smash the peas and serve with the meat. The addition of one-half pound flour and two quarts of the liquor [broth], boiled 10 minutes, makes a great improvement. Add six sliced onions, fried, to make it very delicate (Rywell, ed., 1861 Army Cookbook, recipe 2A).

100 pounds pork, divided in 2 lots
24 pounds peas, divided into 4 lots, wrapped in 4 pudding cloths
2 teaspoonsful pepper
½ pound flour
2 quarts liquor [this means broth, not alcohol!]
6 sliced onions, fried

Plain Irish Stew for Fifty Men

Cut fifty pounds of mutton into pieces of one-quarter pound each, put them in a pan, add eight pounds of large onions, twelve pounds of whole potatoes, eight tablespoonsful of salt, three tablespoonsful of pepper, and cover all with water, giving about one-half pint to each pound. Then light the fire; 1-½ hours of gentle ebullition will make a most excellent stew. Mash some of the potatoes to thicken the gravy and serve. Dumplings may be added at one-half hour before done (Rywell, recipe 5).

Suet Dumplings

Take one-half pound of flour, one-half a teaspoon salt, one-quarter teaspoon pepper, one-quarter pound of chopped fat pork or beef suet, eight tablespoons of water, and mix well together to form a thick paste. When formed, divide paste into six or eight pieces and roll in flour. Boil with the meat for 20 to 30 minutes. A little chopped onion or aromatic herbs will give it a flavor (Rywell, recipe 21).

Turkish Pilaf for One Hundred Men

Put in the cauldron two pounds of fat which you have saved from salt pork and add to it four pounds of peeled and sliced onions. Let them fry in the fat for about 10 minutes. Add in twelve pounds of rice; cover the rice with water, the rice

being submerged two inches, and add to it seven tablespoons salt and one of pepper. Let simmer gently for about
1 hour, stirring it with a spatula occasionally to prevent
burning. When commencing to boil, a very little fire ought
to be kept under. Each grain ought to be swollen to the full
size of rice, and separate. On a different stove, put fat and
onions in equal quantities with the same seasoning.

Cut the flesh of the mutton, veal, pork, or beef from
the bone, cut in dice of about two ounces each. Put in pan
with fat and onions, setting it going with a very sharp fire,
having put in two quarts of water. Steam gently, stirring
occasionally for about half an hour, till forming a rather
thick rich gravy. When both the rice and meat are done,
mix together and serve. Any kind of vegetables may be
frizzled with the onions (Rywell, recipe 8).

The next three recipes come from Mrs. Annie Wittenmyer's book, *A Collection of Recipes for the Use of Special Diet
Kitchens in Military Hospitals*, 1864:

Broiled Mackerel

Soak [mackerel] in cold water several hours, rub in a little
butter and pepper, and broil over a slow fire. [Salted mackerel came in wooden tubs in brine. Salt cod and finnan
haddie (smoked haddock) were commonly eaten throughout
America in the nineteenth century] (Wittenmyer, 14).

Stewed Oysters

For each pint of oysters, place over the fire one pint of milk,
add the juice of the oysters, a spoonful of butter, and a little
pepper and salt, and two pounded crackers. Let it come to
a boil, add the oysters, and let it simmer 5 minutes
(Wittenmyer, 15).

Indian Meal Pudding

A favorite dessert at military posts, [I]ndian pudding takes a long time to bake, but is simple to put together.

Into four quarts of milk, stir one-half teacup of suet, chopped fine. Place it over a fire till it comes to a boil; set off, sift and stir into this enough meal to make a thin batter; let it cool, then dredge in one tablespoonful flour; season with salt, sugar and spices to taste (ginger, cinnamon, nutmeg, or mace). Remember that meal becomes sweeter by baking. Bake 3 to 4 hours, with steady but not large fire (Wittenmyer, 19).

Spruce Beer

Bottled beer was late in coming West, due to the difficulties of keeping bottles of unpasteurized beer from blowing up. But wherever there was a military base, beer was a necessity, and if there was no nearby brewery, very often men made their own. An old-time American favorite that has fallen out of favor is spruce beer. It was both tasty and easy to make. Moreover, spruce beer was considered more healthy than spirits, and it had a reputation for being a good preventative of scurvy. It was popular during the American Revolution.

Recipe for Spruce Beer

2 quarts young spruce sprigs
4 ounces hops
½ gallon molasses
2–3 ounces essence spruce
2 ounces yeast
water

Essence: Make essence of spruce by boiling young tender sprigs of spruce in three gallons of water for 3 hours. Strain, discard the spruce, and keep the water. Repeat procedure with new spruce in old spruce water, and repeat a third time. Strain and save liquid essence of spruce.

To Make Beer: Boil hops 30 minutes in gallon of water. Use only one quart of this liquid and combine with molasses, two to three ounces of spruce extract, and four gallons of warm water. Pour it into a freshly cleaned cask and add yeast. Shake well and allow to stand 10 to 14 days. Do *NOT put bung in barrel, or the fermentation will blow it out. [Modern wine-making shops carry air locks to allow gases to escape without oxygen entering] (Farmer, The King's Bread, 2nd Rising, 50).*

Nobody seems to know the origin of the name "St. Jacob's soup," but the recipe came down to us from Benjamin Morgan Roberts, a member of the Mormon Battalion, which came along the Santa Fe Trail in 1846 during the Mexican War.

St. Jacob's Soup

Cut pork in small pieces and cook till light brown. In another pot, cook potatoes and onions until tender; add pork with some of the fat, and tomatoes. Simmer for 12 minutes and serve with toasted croutons over the top (Carter, ed., The Pioneer Cookbook, 24).

¼ pound salt pork
2 good-sized potatoes, diced
2 onions, sliced
4 fresh tomatoes

Two other Mormon favorites were "finker" and "colcannon," hearty pioneer dishes probably brought by the "Saints" from Europe.

Finker

Grind cracklings with liver and heart, mixing all well. Then, mix with apples, onions, salt, and pepper. Cook in a frying pan until liver is just cooked and all is hot. Serve as a meat dish with warm cooked vegetables. (Recipe collection of Sam Arnold.)

1 pound pork kidney fat, rendered to cracklings
1 pound calf liver
1 pound boiled beef heart
2 apples, peeled and diced
2 yellow onions, peeled and diced
salt and pepper to taste

6 peeled potatoes
½ pound fresh cleaned spin-
    ach
1 tablespoon butter
salt and pepper to taste

Colcannon

*Cook potatoes and spinach separately. Drain, mash pota-
toes, and chop dried spinach fine. Mix with butter, salt, and
pepper, and place in a greased mold. Give it 10 minutes in
a hot oven, 375º F., then unmold and serve (Carter, 27).*

References

Arnold, Sam. *Frying Pans West.* 11th ed. Denver: Arnold & Company, 1985.

Carter, Kate B., ed. *The Pioneer Cookbook.* Salt Lake City: Daughters of Utah Pioneers, 1961.

Clarke, Dwight L. *Stephen Watts Kearny, Soldier of the West.* Norman: University of Oklahoma Press, 1961.

Cooke, Philip St. George. *Scenes and Adventures in the Army; or Romance of Military Life.* Philadelphia: Lindsay and Blakiston, 1857.

Farmer, Dennis and Carol. *The King's Bread, 2nd Rising: Cooking at Niagara (1726–1815).* Youngstown, N.Y.: Old Fort Niagara Association, Inc., 1989.

Fort Larned. Soldier's letter dated April 9, 1867.

Frazer, Robert W. *Forts of the West.* Norman: University of Oklahoma Press, 1972.

Grierson, Alice Kirk. *An Army Wife's Cookbook, With Household Hints and Home Remedies.* Edited by Mary L. Williams. Globe, Ariz.: Southwest Parks and Monuments Association, 1972.

McCall, Colonel George Archibald. *New Mexico in 1850: A Military View.* Edited by Robert W. Frazer. Norman: University of Oklahoma Press, 1968.

Rickey, Don, Jr. *Forty Miles a Day on Beans and Hay.* Norman: University of Oklahoma Press, 1963 (reference to soldier's rations, 248–249).

Rywell, Martin, ed. *1861 Army Cookbook.* Harriman, Tenn.: Pioneer Press, 1956.

Simmons, Marc. *Following the Santa Fe Trail.* Santa Fe: Ancient City Press, 1984.

Wittenmyer, Mrs. Annie. *A Collection of Recipes for the Use of Special Diet Kitchens in Military Hospitals, 1864.* Edited by Sara Jackson and J. M. Carrol. Mattituck, N.Y.: J. M. Carrol & Co., 1983.

Chapter 6

The Fur Traders and Bent's Fort

After crossing southwest through Kansas and meeting the Arkansas River, travelers had a choice of two routes to Santa Fe. The longer and safer "Mountain Branch" followed the Arkansas River west across southern Colorado to Bent's Fort and then veered diagonally southwest along Timpas Creek to Raton Pass. Once over the difficult mountains, the open plains stretched out to the south, and you were about six days' journey from Santa Fe. The alternate route was called the Cimarron cutoff. In eastern Colorado, the trail left the Arkansas River and traveled across a desolate, generally waterless route southwest. It was faster, but harder on the stock and more dangerous. Attacks by Comanches, Apaches, and other tribes were common. Despite its dangers, the Cimarron cutoff became the preferred route to Santa Fe, superseding the mountain branch, which had been favored from 1824 to 1835.

In the early 1830s, the beaver-fur trade in the mountains was still thriving, and fur companies built trade forts at strategic points along the trail to supply both free and company trappers and to provide goods for the Indian trade.

From 1824 to 1846, the Arkansas River served as the border between the United States and Mexico. It was logical that Missouri traders Charles and William Bent, along with their St. Louis partner, Ceran St. Vrain, built a huge adobe trading fort on the north side of the Arkansas River, near the place where the wagon trains crossed into Mexico (present-day

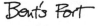

Bent's Fort

La Junta, Colorado). Begun in 1834 and completed in 1835, this huge adobe citadel, called Bent's Fort, stood next to the Santa Fe Trail about sixty miles east of the Rockies. It was the region's most important center for the fur-trade and buffalo-hide business, and it became the hub of a vast commercial empire that reached from present-day Amarillo, Texas, on the east to the Gila River on the west and Fort Laramie, Wyoming, in the north.

Within the thick adobe walls lived some sixty employees of Bent, St. Vrain & Company. The staff, headed by William Bent, was heavily New Mexican. Alexander Barclay, an English bookkeeper at the fort for some years, lent an air of sophistication to the frontier company. Dick Green and his wife, Charlotte, "queen of the kitchen," were black slaves of William Bent.

On any day, in the courtyard, you would have been likely to meet scruffy, buckskin-clad mountain men, French-Canadian trappers, Missouri-twanged mule-drivers, ox teamsters, odorous buffalo skinners, a German or English tourist, an Irishman in U.S. soldier's uniform, and, probably, several southern Cheyenne or Arapahoe Indians. Mexico, just across the river, was the land of the *vaquero* (cowboy) and the *cibolero* (buffalo hunter), the Comanche and Apache, and, often, hostile Mexican officials. The Southern Cheyennes and their brothers, the Arapahoes, had close relations with the Bents. William, in fact, was married to a fine Cheyenne lady named Owl Woman.

From its giant American flag, boasting twenty-seven stars at the time, to its lemonade and mint julep "hailstorms," Bent's Fort offered a welcome haven for trappers, traders, travelers, soldiers, and tradesmen alike. It was the western outpost of American civilization, and this fact was reflected in its food and drink.

The Mexican employees at Bent's Fort tended horses, a few cattle, sheep, goats, and even three buffalo calves at one time. They also cared for the many barnyard fowl, including two peacocks, termed "thunderbirds" by the Indians, due to their loud squawking. The fowl and livestock provided a wide variety of meats, although the English bookkeeper Alexander Barclay groused bitterly about the sameness of the foods:

> If ever they chanced to kill a beast while out somewhere nearer home than common, they dispatched two of the fellows with mules and allowed us the luxury of a little fresh

meat. The dried meat retains its dry hard quality when cooked, not being in any manner cured, but cut in slices like thick steaks before drying. Vegetables they have none. Of farinacious matters . . . wheat flour and Indian corn meal make our bread, but thence as circumstances allow us to get them here. We are, however, never without one or the other.

Coffee and through the summer, milk is plentifull [sic] having four cows and a great many goats which constitute the extent of our larder. The dried meat is put into a skillet and fried in fat. This is their invariable way of cooking and they have no desire to learn any other. However, this is second nature and I suppose, when I get well, custom will reconcile me to it. Were the fare only increased by the addition of potatoes, I could be well content, but the soil is so miserably poor it will not even produce them (Barclay, letter dated October 15, 1838).

The absence of potatoes remains something of a mystery, for we find references in the Bent, St. Vrain inventories of "potatoes in barrels" going west. Whether these potatoes were to be eaten or used for planting, we do not know. In Santa Fe, there were several newspaper mentions of the lack of potatoes in the west. (The term "Murpheys" was used for Irish potatoes, especially among the military.)

Inside Bent's Old Fort
toward the kitchen

Barclay's lament continues:

We brought up two young pigs and they are prospering mightily, being a great deal of waste about the fort. Four turkeys and about 30 fowls constitute all the livestock on which one can expect to draw for provisions. I rather expect they will keep a few sheep next summer as they are to be bought very cheap in the Spanish country beyond the mountains. Our chief dependence here is on the buffalo for meat which are generally to be found within 15–30 miles of the fort (Barclay, letter dated October 15, 1838).

Although Barclay's comments, made in 1838 (about four years after the fort was first in operation), indicated that Bent's Fort wasn't much of a gourmet paradise, there seem to have been subsequent improvements. The lists of foodstuffs brought west by the Bent, St. Vrain & Company in later years include lemon syrup for lemonade, bottles of lime juice, Yung Hyson tea from China, and Bent's Water Biscuits, made by the Bent brothers' cousins in Milton, Massachusetts, and a point of pride for the family because the Bent name was stamped on each of the bone-dry, white, wheat-flour biscuits.

In charge of the kitchen at Bent's Fort for a number of years was Charlotte, wife of Charles Bent's slave, Dick Green. English writer and western traveler George Frederick Ruxton wrote of Charlotte, "Over the culinary department presided of late years a fair lady of colour, Charlotte by name, who was, as she loved to say, 'de onlee lady in de dam Injun country,' and who moreover was celebrated from Longs Peak to the Cumbres Espanolas for slapjacks and pumpkin pies" (Ruxton, *Life in the Far West,* 180).

Pumpkin Pie (from an old recipe)

Mix dry ingredients together, then fold in eggs with whisk. Add pumpkin and whisk well. Add the milk and mix in. Pour into a 10-inch pie shell and bake [at 350° F.] for 1 hour and 25 minutes. Serve with whipped cream or ice cream. (Recipe collection of Sam Arnold.)

1-½ cups sugar
½ teaspoon salt
1-¼ teaspoons cinnamon
2 eggs
2 cups pumpkin puree [cooked fresh pumpkin, beaten; or canned]
1-¼ cups milk

Slap Jacks

Take and scald a quart of Indian meal in milk, if you have it — water will do. Turn it out and stir in a half pint of flour, half a pint of yeast [a package of dry yeast in a cup of warm water], and a little salt. Fry them, when light, in just sufficient fat to keep them from sticking to the frying pan. Another nice way: turn a quart of boiling milk or water to a pint of Indian meal, stir in three [table]spoonsful of flour, three eggs, and two teaspoons of salt (Webster, 132).

In his *New Mexico Report, 1846–1847*, Lieutenant James W. Abert tells of an unusual pickle made from the *Myrtinia proboscidia* (Devil's Claw), a weed that grows in the vicinity of Bent's Fort. He wrote, "We also had today, some pickles of the wild Myrtinia which grow abundant about the Fort. They appear to me to resemble the okra very much, and I doubt not would be good to use for the same purposes" (*Abert's New Mexico Report*, 10).

Pickled Devil's Claws (to make one gallon)

85 devil's claw pods, picked young
1 quart white vinegar
3 tablespoons salt
1 quart fresh water
6 fresh garlic cloves
2 tablespoons black peppercorns
6 bay leaves
2 tablespoons mustard seed
4 whole dried red chile pequin (a small, hot chile)
2 sprigs fresh dill

Bring water, vinegar, and salt to boil. Add other spices and herbs. Pack cleaned, washed pods, with a knife-prick in each, into a wide-mouthed gallon jar which has been sterilized with boiling water. Add dill sprigs. Pour boiling pickling liquid over pods in jar. Fill and seal. Note: Pick devil's claw pods in late July or early August. It's important to pick them young, before the skeleton inside the pod and antenna has formed and hardened. If hardened, the sharp hook at the end of the antenna may cut your mouth. When eating, have a care, as it is difficult for the picker to be sure that the pod's interior is completely soft. They are excellent, and in 1989, Dexter Hess, a botanist/historian, produced eight gallons of superb devil's claw pickles. (I learned this recipe from Dexter Hess.)

Good Times and Fandango

While life at Bent's Fort was hard, it was not without its pleasures. During his visit to Bent's Fort in the winter of 1846–47, teenager Lewis Garrard describes an evening of music and dancing:

> . . . myself with numbed fingers gradually thawing in the long, low, dining room, drinking hot coffee, eating bread, buffler, and 'State doins,' and listening to Charlotte, the glib-tongued, sable fort cook, retailing her stock of news and surmises, (it was only then) did I feel entirely free to throw off care (Garrard, 73).

> Rosalie, a half-breed French and Indian squaw (the wife of Ed, the carpenter), and Charlotte, the culinary divinity, were, as a Missouri teamster remarked, "The only female women here." They nightly were led to the floor "to trip the light fantastic toe," swung rudely and gently in the mazes of the contradance — but such a medly of steps is seldom seen out of the mountains — the halting, irregular march of the war dance; the slipping gallopade, the boisterous pitching of the Missouri backwoodsman, and the more nice gyrations of the Frenchmen — for all, irrespective of rank, age and color, went pell mell into the excitement, in a manner that would have rendered a leveler of aristocracies and select companies frantic with delight. It was a most complete democratic demonstration. And then the airs assumed by the fair ones — more particularly Charlotte, who took pattern from real life in the "States," she acted her part to perfection. The grand center of attraction, the belle of the evening, she treated the suitors for the "pleasure of the next set," with becoming ease and suavity of manner. She knew her worth, and managed accordingly; and, when the favored gallant stood by her side, waiting for the rudely-scraped tune from a screaking [sic] violin, satisfaction, joy and triumph over his rivals, were pictured on his radiant face (Garrard, 74).

Wine at Bent's Fort

From the archeological studies and the inventory lists, we have learned that ports and Bordeaux wines were served at the fort. Two Bordeaux wine bottles were found, one containing a glass seal reading "Pauillac Medoc" and the other a seal reading "St. Julien Medoc." The Bent, St. Vrain & Company's inventories also frequently list clarets.

St. Louis newspapers of the period commonly advertised Tenerife red wine, named for the capital city of the largest of the Canary Islands, where the wine originated. Tenerife still produces wine, but it is almost totally consumed locally. It is likely that the Canary Island wine was consumed at Bent's Fort. Madeira, port, and sherry wines, too, doubtless found their way to Bent's Fort, although we have no record of them there. They were popular in Santa Fe.

During the early nineteenth century, vintners normally sold their wines by the barrel, half hogshead, and hogshead (a hogshead holds sixty-three gallons). Often the hand-blown wine bottles were used solely to bring decanted wine from the barrel to the table. Because hand-blown glass bottles broke so easily, they were frequently included in the purchase of a barrel of wine. Thus, the bottles found at Bent's Fort may not have been filled in France but included empty with the purchase of a barrel of Bordeaux.

As noted in Chapter 2, glass bottles were extremely valuable in New Mexico. In *Down the Santa Fe Trail and Into Mexico*, Susan Magoffin noted:

> They . . . sell eggs, sandias [watermelons], tortillas, grapes and the like. They wish to trade for bottles instead of money. They readily gave 4 bits [$.50] apiece for an empty bottle making a fine profit for the owners. We can buy in the states the filled bottles for 3 or 4 dollars a dozen, drink the liquor and then sell the empty bottles for $6 per dozen (Magoffin, 153).

For sale to trappers and travelers and for the use of the proprietors, the store at Bent's Fort carried such unusual luxuries as balsam bitters, pepper sauce, lemon and lime syrups, butter crackers, Bent's water crackers, candies of various sorts and, most remarkable of all, great blue porcelain jars of pre-

77

served Chinese ginger. Older people today may still remember seeing these blue china ginger-jars, which were carried by lines of vegetable rope passed around necks of the jars. Both stem ginger in syrup and crystalized, sugared ginger were contained in those jars, which are still imported into America from China.

In the winter, Chipita, the general housekeeper, sometimes organized a candy-pulling frolic in which the Bent's Fort laborers and teamsters all took part. It was an important jollification. During the afternoon, the black New Orleans molasses called "long sweet," used in the Indian trade, was boiled, and after supper the people gathered in one of the rooms and pulled the taffy candy. Taffy was a great luxury eagerly eaten by those who could get it.

Molasses Taffy

Place the molasses, water, brown sugar, vinegar, salt, and butter in a heavy saucepan. Bring to a boil, stirring until sugar dissolves. Boil without stirring until the mixture registers 250º – 280º F. on a candy thermometer or forms a hard ball when a little is dropped into cold water. Stir in the baking soda and pour onto a buttered marble slab or heatproof platter. When taffy is cool enough to handle, pull it with both hands to a spread of about 18 inches. Fold the taffy back on itself and continue pulling, twisting slightly until ridges of twists retain their shape (about 15 minutes). Form into a long rope on a surface sprinkled with confectioner's sugar. Cut into bite-sized pieces. Yield: about 1 pound. (Recipe collection of Sam Arnold.)

1 cup unsulphured molasses
½ cup water
1-½ cups dark brown sugar
1-½ tablespoons cider vinegar
¼ teaspoon salt
5 tablespoons butter
⅛ teaspoon baking soda
confectioner's sugar

In 1843, Charles Bent and Ceran St. Vrain wrote a letter to the superintendent of Indian Affairs at St. Louis complaining about the illegal liquor trade. In the letter, they described renegade Americans who had built trading houses near the location of the present city of Pueblo, Colorado. The complaint stated that these men carried on a large trade in Mexican whiskey with the Indians. The Bent, St. Vrain & Company asked the government to establish a military post in that area to control these unlicensed traders. It never happened.

Whether or not the Bent brothers participated in selling liquor to the Indians remains an unresolved question. We do know that they had a bar with a huge slate billiard table in a second story room at the Fort. Across one end of the room ran a counter or bar over which drinkables were served.

In *Bent's Old Fort and Its Builders*, George Bird Grinnell describes the annual Independence Day festivities:

> Just before each 4th of July, a party was always sent up into the hills at the head of the Purgatoire River to gather wild mint for mint juleps to be drunk in honor of the day. For mixing these, ice was brought from the ice house. In those days, this drink was called the Hailstorm. To the employees of the fort, liquor was ever dealt out with a very sparing hand and there is no memory of drink ever causing any trouble among the people of the fort (Grinnell, 29).

2 to 3 ounces whiskey (corn, rye, or bourbon)
1 tablespoon sugar (powdered preferred) or simple sugar syrup
2 sprigs mint
shaved or chipped ice to fill a silver julep cup [I use a wide-mouthed pint Mason Jar]

Hailstorm

Using a spoon, bruise the mint in the cup, mixing with sugar. Add the liquor and ice. If using jar, shake it hard fifty times with the lid screwed on tightly. Then drink it from the jar. If using a julep cup, just muddle it. (I learned this recipe, as drunk in Tennessee and old-time Georgia, from my first wife.)

Wassail, a hot, mulled, spiced red wine served with fragrant baked apples floating in the bowl, was a New England Christmas tradition. We have not yet found a written record of wassail being served anywhere on the Santa Fe Trail, but with the Bent family's New England heritage, the apples brought in barrels to the fort, and the red Medoc wine, it is likely that wassail would have found its way into their cups at Christmas.

Wassail

Heat a large bottle of good red wine, either burgundy or claret. In two other bowls, beat six eggs separately, then fold the yolks into the stiff egg whites. Meanwhile, place the following into one-half cup water in a pan: nutmeg, cloves, ginger, mace, allspice, cinnamon, and sugar. Heat all together to boiling until spices are cooked a bit to release their flavor. Allow to cool and pour the egg mix together with the spices, sugar, and hot red wine into a punch bowl. Place in it the six baked apples and serve. The apples release a delicious flavor into the wassail, a very special holiday drink. (Recipe collection of Sam Arnold.)

1 large bottle burgundy or claret wine
6 eggs, separated
½ cup water
¼ teaspoon nutmeg
2 cloves
½ teaspoon ginger
½ teaspoon mace
½ teaspoon allspice
1 teaspoon cinnamon
2 cups sugar
6 baked apples

Beaver Tail

On the eve of the bloody Sand Creek massacre in Colorado, William Bent served beaver to the visiting military. In his book *The Battle of Sand Creek,* Morse H. Coffin notes:

During the afternoon, by invitation, the lieutenant and sergeants took supper at Col. B's table, which we considered something of an honor. The Colonel himself, did not sup with us, but seated near, engaged us in agreeable conversation. For meat, we were served with beaver, which was a new dish to some, but well liked, I think, by all. The cook was a half breed, (though not a son of Col. B.), and a mortal homely fellow, besides being badly pitted by small pox (Coffin, 16).

I have cooked a number of beaver tails, and find that they are nearly solid gelatin, the same material as fingernails and hooves. If you boil one gently for about 45 minutes at a slow boil, you may, after it cools, remove the thin, black, pebbled skin with a knife. Cut just through the skin around the perimeter with a sharp blade, or a razor, and peel away the skin. The tail may then be breaded and baked, or more often, cut up and used as a thickener for soup. Cooked beaver tail is not unlike the fatty material of a turtle and has only a slight swampy taste. For my money, I prefer the hind-leg hams of the beaver. They are dark meat, like goose flesh, and are good eating.

References

[Abert, Lieutenant James W.] *Abert's New Mexico Report, 1846–47*. Albuquerque: Horn and Wallace, 1962.

Barclay, Alexander. Letter dated October 15, 1838. Bancroft Collection. University of California, Berkeley.

Coffin, Morse H. *The Battle of Sand Creek*. Edited by Alan W. Farley. Waco, Tex.: W. M. Morrison, 1965.

Garrard, Lewis H. *Wah-To-Yah and the Taos Trail*. Norman: University of Oklahoma Press, 1955.

Grinnell, George Bird. *Bent's Old Fort and Its Builders*. Wichita: Kansas Historical Society, 1912 (reference to ginger, 35; to the bar, 111).

Magoffin, Susan Shelby. *Down the Santa Fe Trail and Into Mexico: The Diary of Susan Shelby Magoffin, 1846–1847*. Edited by Stella M. Drumm. New Haven, Conn.: Yale University Press, 1926.

Ruxton, George Frederick. *Life in the Far West*. Edited by Leroy R. Hafen. Norman: University of Oklahoma Press, 1951.

Webster, Mrs. A. L. *The Improved Housewife, or Book of Receipts*. Hartford, Conn.: Ira Webster, 1843.

Chapter 7

From Bent's Fort and on Into New Mexico

Bent's Fort

When Lewis Garrard arrived at Bent's Fort, he sat down to a plate at a table for the first time in fifty days and ate with a knife and fork. Food at this "Citadel of the Prairie" was a treat to the wagon-weary travelers. Refreshing drinks were available, including lemonade, tea, coffee, and a wide variety of wines and spirits.

With the exception of lemonade, no other cold, non-alcoholic drink was reported at Bent's Fort. Because of the many Mexican employees and activities of Bent, St. Vrain & Company in trade with Mexico, it's quite likely that various traditional Mexican cold drinks, called *refrescos*, were prepared: *horchata, agua de arroz, colonche,* and lemonade with chia.

Horchata

7 ounces of melon seeds
1 cup sugar
1-½ quarts water
grated rind of one lemon
crushed ice

Clean the melon seeds, then grind them (a blender is easiest) with water, sugar, and the lemon rind. Let mixture stand 5 hours, then squeeze through a damp tea towel. Serve in tall glasses with crushed ice. It picks up the delicious flavor of the melon seeds, and this will vary according to which melon seeds you use — watermelons were common in New Mexico from earliest days. (Recipe collection of Sam Arnold.)

EATING UP THE SANTA FE TRAIL

"Horchata" is Spanish for orgeat, a refreshing barley water, which the French make by replacing the barley with almonds. Spaniards and Mexicans, who have more melons than almonds, substitute cantaloupe, watermelon, cucumber, and pumpkin seeds for the barley. Today in Mexico you will find a fine cooling drink made of any of these seeds, or all of them put together.

Four-Seed Horchata

Wash seeds thoroughly; grind them fine, shells and all. Stir in water with sugar and cinnamon. Let stand in refrigerator for 2 to 3 days (or as long as you want). Stir from time to time and when all of the delicious seed flavor has been released into the water, strain through a cloth. Add ice and serve. (Recipe collection of Sam Arnold.)

½ cup cantaloupe seeds
½ cup watermelon seeds
½ cup squash seeds
½ cup cucumber seeds
1 quart water
½ cup sugar
dash orange-flower water
2 teaspoons cinnamon

Colonche and Lemonade with Chia

Colonche is a Mexican drink made from the juices of the prickly pear (cactus) fruit sweetened with honey and allowed to stand for twenty-four hours to improve its flavor. The fruit of the prickly pear yields a delicious, sharp red juice similar to that of pomegranate. Colonche is enjoyed in Mexico and was discovered on the South Platte River near present-day Denver by traveler Rufus B. Sage in 1842. He came upon a camp consisting of four lodges, three housing whites and one of Blackfoot Indians who had left the Blackfoot nation to join the Arapahoes living on the South Platte. According to Sage, they had forsaken their own nation because of its uncompromising hostility to the whites. Quite a number of Blackfeet had joined the Sioux and Nez Percés for the same reason. Sage was entertained by the whites and the Indians, who provided him with a variety of colonche:

> Among the delicacies set before us was one deserving of notice . . . it consisted of the fruit of prickly pears (cacti) boiled in water for some 10–12 hours till it became perfectly

soft, when it was compressed through a thin cloth into the fluid into which it boiled. This forms a delicious variety in mountain fare and one highly stimulating and nutritious. The immense quantities of cacti flower found near the mountains . . . renders the above an entertainment not uncommon (Sage, 217).

Chia seed was well known in New Mexico and often used in lemonades. The little sage seeds were first made to pop open by soaking in hot water for 10 minutes. These are then added to fresh lemonade, providing delicious, soft, tapioca-like tiny seeds floating in the drink.

Atole and Chaquehue

Mexican workers frequently ate *atole,* a thin cornmeal gruel. Still much esteemed in Mexico, atole is often sweetened with raw sugar and flavored with fresh fruits such as pineapple or strawberries; or seasoned, sprinkled with chile.

Almond Atole

4 cups milk
1 cup blanched almonds
2 cups water
3 egg yolks
1 cup sugar
3 ounces cornstarch
1 stick cinnamon

Grind one cup of blanched almonds in a little milk. This is easily done in a blender. Dissolve three ounces of cornstarch in two cups of water. Boil together with a stick of cinnamon until thickened. Add one cup of sugar and four cups of milk to the thickened cornstarch and continue cooking until it thickens again. Add the ground almonds and three egg yolks, beaten lightly. Reheat and let mixture come to a boil. Remove and serve immediately. (Recipe collection of Sam Arnold.)

A thicker variety of cornmeal mush is frequently eaten with milk and sugar, or with red chile. It is *chaquehue* (pronounced chaw-kay-hway), which is made with water and toasted, dried, ground corn. The older villagers in northern New Mexico enjoy chaquehue for both breakfast and supper. Often made from blue cornmeal, chaquehue is eaten thick from

EATING UP THE SANTA FE TRAIL

a bowl, or sometimes shaped in a loaf pan and fried on a griddle. (I mix the cooked mush with cooked pork meat, chopped green chile, onion, garlic, and oregano. When it's all cooked, I lay plastic wrap in a loaf pan, pour the mixture in and then cover the top with wrap, too, to keep the chaquehue from forming a dry crust on top. To unmold, simply invert, and the loaf of chaquehue falls into your hand. Slice it off in one-half-inch-thick slices, then fry it on the griddle.) *Mejor que el primero beso!*

In addition to atole made from *masa* (Mexican cornmeal), some varieties were based on ground rice, and others on fresh corn. Normally served hot, atole is highly nourishing, and one soon develops a taste for it. Patients at Santa Fe's St. Vincent's Hospital are still offered atole on the daily menu. Today's Mexican supermarkets sell packaged atole, frequently flavored with artificial vanilla, strawberry, cinnamon, or coconut. Normally, atole is a hearty cornmeal gruel, but the commercial Mexican packaged brands are little more than flavored cornstarch. Atole may be mixed with hot milk in place of the traditional water or broth, and it makes a tasty, sweet, smooth, hot children's beverage.

Pinole

Toasted cornmeal, or masa, may be cooked with water, sugar, and cinnamon to make a thin gruel called *pinole*. With the addition of chocolate, pinole makes an excellent winter drink known as *champurrado*. While no evidence exists that champurrado was served at Bent's Fort, both the masa and the chocolate were available, and it is more than likely that Chipita, the general housekeeper, served pinole and champurrado to the many children at the fort. Here is the recipe:

86

Champurrado

Toast in a frying pan one-half cup masa harina (ground hominy corn). Mix it with one cup cold water in a saucepan or bowl. Place mixture in an earthenware pot with one-and-one-half cups of boiling water. Cook about 15 minutes, stirring, until the corn is softened and makes a thin gruel. Add a large square of Mexican chocolate (if available) or sweet dark chocolate, plus a little extra brown sugar to sweeten. Add one-half teaspoon ground cinnamon or several cinnamon sticks and stir until thickened. Pour into cups and serve with a spoon. It can be drunk like hot chocolate or eaten like a thin soup. (Recipe collection of Sam Arnold.)

Mexican Pot Coffee

For each cup of coffee, boil one cup of water in an olla (earthenware pot). Obtain some coarsely ground espresso or dark roasted coffee. For each cup, add one tablespoon coffee to the earthenware pot, plus a stick of cinnamon and dark brown sugar. (In Mexican groceries, you will find little "pillars" of raw brown sugar called piloncillos. *These were and still are used for sweetening. Sometimes they are called* panochas *after their use in making* panocha, *a dessert pudding made with sprouted wheat flour.) (Recipe collection of Sam Arnold.)*

Taos Lightning

To those participating in the alcohol trade with Indians, the routes west were blocked by federal troops. Enterprising Americans therefore took stills across the border to New Mexico, which was under Mexican rule until 1846. There, they could operate with no moralistic government interference. While no records have been found indicating the volume of alcohol produced in Taos and other areas of northern New Mexico, there were at least five distilleries in the Taos area at the time of the Mexican War in the summer of 1846. The first was built in 1825 in a canyon close to San Fernandez by James Baird, Peg-leg Smith, and a man named Stevens. In *Wah-To-Yah and the Taos Trail*, Lewis Garrard quotes a mountain man who disparages the quality of Taos whiskey:

> "Wagh!" chimed in a hardy self-pleased mountain man, "this knocks the hind sights off of Touse [Taos whiskey]. I'se drunk . . . a heap liquor in my chargin' lifetime. Thar's alkyhol as makes drunk came mity quick; but 't ain't good — burns up the innards; an' a feller feels like a gut-shot coyote. Then thar's Touse arwardenty; it's d——d poor stuff — kin taste the corn in it — makes me think I'm a hos, a feedin' away fur plowin' time; an' I allers squeals, an' raises my hind foot to kick, when any palou comes about my heels" (Garrard, 199–200).

According to Josiah Gregg, an American trader to Mexico, a new type of high-yield wheat had been brought from "Chi-hua-hua" into northern New Mexico around 1810. From this strain of wheat, grain distillers made their mash and produced a "Taos Lightning," or aguardiente. Shipped in small cotton-wood kegs, this potent spirit became a major trade item to the Indians as far north as Wyoming, and possibly beyond. The Richard brothers, who operated a trading post near Fort Laramie, made regular trips to Taos to bring back the whiskey.

In January 1847, Charles Bent, who became the first American governor of the Territory of New Mexico, was murdered by a mob during a general insurrection against American rule. The ring-leaders were captured by the American forces and hanged in Taos. After the hanging, the mountain men congregated at Estis's Tavern, where one of the most-requested drinks was eggnog. One mountain man remembers:

> Shouldering our rifles, we walked to the tavern — discussing the length of time a man will live after he is swung off — where the fellows, washing, primed with the "raw" (real American brandy, from Estis' personal store, less adulterated than that at the bar), and seating themselves in the family

New Mexico maiden

room, near the handsome senors, were regaled with the best egg nog it is possible to manufacture from the materials (Garrard, 199).

Taos Hanging Eggnog

2 dozen egg yolks
1 cup sugar
1 bottle strong brandy

Beat the egg yolks for a long time until fluffy and creamy. Add sugar gradually to taste. Add brandy and fold into beaten yolk mix. Mixture may be flavored with a little vanilla or cinnamon, if you like. This recipe keeps in the refrigerator almost indefinitely, as the alcohol "pickles" the egg yolks. (Recipe collection of Sam Arnold.)

A "noggin" was a small, round, birchwood cylinder made into a drinking container. Noggins were used at the table, while tankards were used at the bar. An American bachelor in Santa Fe in the 1840s reported that they made their eggnogs by putting a Spanish primer over a glass with sugar, whiskey, and an egg and then shaking the glass vigorously. One wonders about the specific book mentioned; it served to hold the eggnog in the glass — was it supposed to impart a Spanish flavor as well?

Here's my favorite recipe for an old-time eggnog (you won't find it offered by dairies in paper cartons):

Old-Time Eggnog

12 eggs
1 cup sugar
½ quart bottle Jamaican rum
1 quart bourbon
1 quart whipping cream
1 quart milk
nutmeg

Separate eggs and beat yolks till yellow and whites till stiff. Add sugar to yolks and beat in. Mix egg yolks and sugar in large punch bowl with rum, bourbon, and milk. Fold in the egg whites along with the beaten whipped cream. Top with nutmeg. It is rich, potent, and as delicious as the first kiss (Arnold, 71).

Corn-Sugar Molasses

Molasses, made either from sugarcane or corn syrup, was a staple in early nineteenth-century America. Sugarcane molasses, often called long sweet, was brought to Bent's Fort and Santa Fe by the Bent, St. Vrain & Company wagons. It was used in cooking and was combined with vinegar to make a common drink called switchel. The New Mexicans made a type of sweet molasses from corn stalks (corn syrup), which tasted different from molasses made from sugarcane. In Abert's *New Mexico Report*, the process of making corn-sugar molasses is described:

> It being the season for making molasses, they were all busy in laying in a winter supply. . . . They cut the stock of the maize, or Indian corn, and, after stripping it of the leaves, pound it with heavy wooden mallets until it is reduced to a pulp; after steaming it sufficiently, they express the juice by means of a rude press, and then evaporate it to the proper consistency in earthen jars (*Abert's New Mexico Report*, 60–61).

❖ ❖ ❖

The summer of 1846, when General Kearny's invasion force marched into New Mexico, was dry and hot. The crops were poor, and the Americans found little forage for their animals. Hard cash was also scarce, and the native New Mexicans weren't pleased to have to take paper scrip from the invading army.

After endless miles of trail, at last Kearny's men arrived at a town. It was called Las Vegas, named for the fields where crops were grown. Here, he brought the town officials and the priest near to him as he assured the New Mexicans that their religion and their property would not be taken from them.

On they marched to San Miguel del Vado, crossing the river and entering the town, which was dominated by a fine church. Then, they moved on to Old Pecos, where the remains of an old Spanish church mouldered by a huge, deserted Indian pueblo. It was said that in the past, a mammoth rattlesnake was kept at the pueblo in an underground kiva, and Indian babies were fed to it.

Finally, Kearny's men arrived in Santa Fe. After such a long trip, the soldiers' beards were removed or trimmed and baths taken at La Barberia, a rancho on the trail, a few hours' journey outside of town. Lotions, hair dressing, and perfumes replaced the trail dirt as the soldiers prepared for the "big doin's" awaiting them in town.

Compared to their American counterparts, New Mexican women had low-cut blouses and shorter skirts, showing leg and ankle. Often, to keep their skin as light as possible, they wore rice-powder paste on their faces, which made them look like corpses. At fandango, which happened nearly every night, the New Mexican women gave their American dancing partners a friendly welcome. The clothing, cosmetics, and "liberal" behavior shocked the young soldiers coming from a Victorian land, but it took only a moment to adjust and admire the view.

After the grand victory ball held in Santa Fe, troopers, including Lieutenant Abert, headed south toward Albuquerque. Here is his description of Bernalillo. He saw

> some pretty donacellas plucking the fruit. They had round, flat looking baskets placed on their heads; these were piled with thick-clustered bunches of the purple grape, from beneath which the bright black eyes of the donacellas were sparkling. We could not pass by such a beautiful vineyard, so we stopped and asked for some fruit; some of the maidens, with merry faces, came toward us, when they were suddenly stopped by the gruff voice of a man crying out, that he would himself bring the the grapes (*Abert's New Mexico Report, 72*).

Wine Production in El Paso

Although Santa Fe was the terminus of the Santa Fe Trail, soldiers and mountain men, merchants and traders, soon realized that it was not the end of the road. Santa Fe was also the beginning of an even longer road, the Camino Real (royal road) to old Mexico. American trade goods found their way as far south as Mexico City. Far to the south of Albuquerque lay the community of El Paso (now part of Texas) where the Rio Grande took a southeast turn. The town was famed for its delicious wine and brandy. One visitor noted:

> The most important production of the valley is grapes, from which are annually manufactured not less than "two hundred thousand gallons of perhaps the richest and best wine in the world." This wine is worth two dollars per gallon, and

Mountain Man
Based on
John Harrington

constitutes the principal revenue of the city. The El Paso wines are superior in richness and flavor and pleasantness to taste to anything in the United States, and I doubt not that they are far superior to the best wines ever produced in the Valley of the Rhine or on the sunny hills of France. Also a great quantity of the grapes of this valley are dried in clusters and preserved for use through the winter. . . . I regard them far superior to the best raisins that are imported into the United States (W.W.H. Davis, *El Gringo, or New Mexico and Her People*, 379–380).

References

[Abert, Lieutenant James W.] *Abert's New Mexico Report, 1846–47*. Albuquerque: Horn and Wallace, 1962.

Davis, W.W.H. *El Gringo, or New Mexico and Her People*. Harper and Brothers, 1857. Reprint. Lincoln: University of Nebraska Press, 1982.

Garrard, Lewis H. *Wah-To-Yah and the Taos Trail*. Norman: University of Oklahoma Press, 1955.

Gregg, Josiah. *Commerce of the Prairies*. Vol. 1. New York: Henry G. Langley, 1844. Reprint. Keystone Western Americana Series. Edited by Archibald Hanna and William H. Goetzmann. New York and Philadelphia: J. J. Lippincott Company, 1962.

Sage, Rufus B. *Rocky Mountain Life, or Startling Scenes and Perilous Adventure, in the Far West*. Dayton, Ohio: Edward Canby, 1846.

Chapter 8

Spaniard, Mexican, and Indian

While Santa Fe, by 1840, had engaged in trade with the States for nearly two decades, and American foods and alcohols were sold in town, a gentle farm/rancho life still existed in many areas. Places such as the Rancho de las Golandrinas, a few miles south of Santa Fe, and the fine Rio Grande pueblos of San Juan, San Ildefonso, Santa Clara, Santo Domingo, San Felipe, and Cochiti all kept the old traditions alive. Here are some of the foods served at the ranches and pueblos:

Machaca de Huevo

A delicious, typical breakfast and supper dish found in New Mexico and the northern Mexican province of Chihuahua is machaca de huevo, a combination of beaten jerky, eggs, and chiles. The jerky may be toasted in the oven until a little crisp, and then pounded, although some cooks omit the pounding. When the shreds of meat are ready, a small tomato is fried with some minced onion and two fresh, green, small serrano chiles, finely minced. The beef is added and fried a minute or two longer. Next, two eggs are broken over the top and stirred into the beef, tomato, and chile mixture. Use one cup of jerky for two people. (Recipe collection of Sam Arnold.)

Sopa de Vermicelli

Sopa de vermicelli, or vermicelli soup, a dish reported by Susan Magoffin, was one of the "dry" soups of Mexico. A dry soup is a dish cooked with liquid, most of which is absorbed by pasta or rice during cooking. It generally has the consistency of a moist casserole rather than what we traditionally think of as soup.

Fine vermicelli is lightly turned in hot oil and then laid into a baking dish interspersed with a mixture of fried onions and chiles. Small, green tomatillos (small round tomatoes with a paper-like shell on the outside) may be added as well. The whole is swamped in chicken broth and set in the oven to bake for approximately 90 minutes at 325º F.

Because it was easy to make, filling, and tasty, pasta was found in New Mexico in many forms. A variation on the sopa de vermicelli is to remove the cover just before serving and sprinkle with cheese (such as Monterey Jack or cheddar). Allow the cheese to melt over the vermicelli, which should have absorbed the chicken broth almost entirely. Garnish with green and black olives and a pinch or two of coarsely ground red chile. A moment in a hot oven will brown this to a turn. Avocado slices may also be used as a garnish, although they were not reported at Bent's Fort and likely had not come north of Chihuahua or El Paso del Norte (now El Paso, Texas).

Mistela

Mistela, a traditional old New Mexican Christmas drink, uses a wild parsley herb called *chimajá.* Gathered by older people in the Sangre de Cristo mountains near Santa Fe, this herb has a pungent, somewhat medicinal flavor. To make mistela, follow this recipe:

Recipe for Mistela

Simmer spices, sugar, and fruit together in water for 30 minutes. Strain and add the resulting tea to one gallon of whiskey. As the tea has a strong flavor, add less than one half of it to the whiskey and gradually strengthen to taste. Chimajá can be too flavorful, in which case, another gallon

½ cup chimajá
1 pound sugar
4 cinnamon sticks
6 cloves
2 cups water
1 gallon whiskey
2 dried orange peels
1 cup sultana raisins
½ cup peeled whole
  almonds

of whiskey is called for. In the old days mistela was served warm at Christmas in small cups. Being deliciously strong, it needs careful attention. (Recipe collection of Sam Arnold.)

Chimajá Whiskey

One tablespoonful of chimajá (a member of the parsley family) per quart of whiskey, allowed to steep for a week at least, gives an aperitif said to be good for stomach trouble. Chimajá whiskey was reported to have been in every New Mexican bar before 1850 (Curtin, Healing Herbs of the Upper Rio Grande, 65–66).

Licor de Yerba Buena

A liqueur called licor de yerba buena (creme de menthe) refreshed early-day New Mexican army-post bachelors at Fort Union. It was made by steeping one pound of bruised mint leaves, peels of five lemons, and four pounds of sugar in one quart of brandy and three pints of water. Add one-half dram of oil of peppermint, if you like that combination with the natural spearmint flavor. Let liquid steep for 2 weeks, strain, and bottle. (Today, a finishing liquid, such as glycerin, is added to give thickness or viscosity to most liqueurs. Any pharmacy can supply it.) (Recipe collection of Sam Arnold.)

The basic cookie made in New Mexico is the *biscochito*, or a little biscuit, also spelled "bizcochito" in the old days. These popular anise-flavored shortbreads are an important part of the New Mexican Christmas food tradition. Biscochitos are served at Indian dances at the pueblos after Mass on Christmas, accompanied by good coffee made with Indian well-water. Both Hispanics and Native Americans make and consume these delightful anise cookies.

Biscochitos

Sift sugar, flour, cinnamon, and anise together; to the cold lard add egg yolk followed by the dry ingredients. Mix well, put into bowls, and place in a cold refrigerator for one-half hour. Roll out and cut into rounds or rectangles. Brush with egg-white wash mixed with a little brandy or rum. Sprinkle little candies on top if desired, or bake plain in a 375º F. oven until golden. (Recipe collection of Sam Arnold.)

2 cups sugar
4 ounces cinnamon
2 cups lard (1 pound)
4 cups flour
1 tablespoon anise seed
1 dozen egg yolks
egg-white wash
brandy or rum

Plaza & Palace of Governors - Santa Fe 1840's
End of the Santa Fe Trail

The traditional New Mexico *sopaipilla* (from *sopaipa*, a fritter soaked in honey) is not normally found in Mexico, except in a flatter form called a *buñuelo*. Both are eaten for dessert. Although the origin of sopaipillas is not known, Mexican buñuelos may have cross-pollinated with Native American fried bread. (Plains Indian fried bread is very much the same as Pueblo or Navajo fried bread: a yeast or baking-powder bread dough rolled out, cut into squares or shaped into rounds, and then fried until puffed up and browned all over.)

Here are recipes for sopaipillas. The one secret to success is quickly spooning very hot fat over the dough while frying to make it puff up:

Sopaipillas Made with Yeast

1 cup less 2 tablespoons warm water (105° F.– 115°F.)
1 package active dry yeast
3 tablespoons sugar
1-¼ teaspoons salt
1 egg
2 tablespoons shortening
3 cups all-purpose flour
fat for frying
honey

Rinse a medium-sized bowl with hot water. Measure the warm water into it. Sprinkle in yeast. Add sugar and salt. Stir until all are thoroughly dissolved. Beat egg and add shortening and half of the flour. Beat hard 2 minutes or until smooth. (Use a wooden spoon or electric mixer at medium speed.) With hands, work remaining flour into dough. Continue working until dough is smooth and elastic. Place dough in a greased bowl. Turn dough over to grease top of dough. Cover bowl with a damp cloth or several thicknesses of plastic wrap. Let dough rise in refrigerator at least 2 hours, or until doubled in bulk. Punch it down. Keep covered up to 4 days, punching down once a day. Use as needed. One-fourth of the dough makes about twelve sopaipillas as follows:

Remove one-quarter of dough from refrigerator. On a well-floured surface, roll it out between one-eighth- and one-quarter-inch thick. Cut into two-inch squares. (Sopaipillas are often irregular in shape, so do not reroll irregular edges. Use these pieces as they are.) Heat fat to between 375° F. and 400°F., or until almost smoking. Fry sopaipillas a few at a time, spooning hot fat over them and turning until puffed and light brown on both sides. Drain on paper towels. Serve with honey. To eat: Bite off a corner. Pour honey into hollow (The Española Valley Cookbook, 40).

Sopaipillas Made with Baking Powder

Into a large bowl, sift together flour, baking powder, dry milk, and salt. Work in the lard and enough lukewarm water to make a soft dough. Refrigerate until ready to use. Then, on a floured surface, roll dough out until it is about one-quarter-inch thick. Cut into two-to-three-inch squares. Heat at least one-and-one-half-inches oil in a heavy skillet or deep fat fryer to 380°F., or until almost smoking. Drop pieces of dough a few at a time into hot fat. Quickly spoon hot fat over dough. They will puff immediately. Turn to brown the other side. Drain on paper towels. Serve at once. To eat: Break open and pour in honey. Makes about two dozen (The Española Valley Cookbook, 40).

4 cups all-purpose flour
4 teaspoons baking powder
12 tablespoons nonfat dry milk
1-½ teaspoons salt
1 tablespoon lard
lukewarm water
fat for frying
honey

Honey

Honeybees were originally brought from England to the Americas. With the exception of certain indigenous wasp-like insects that produced a type of honey in Mexico and California, there was no honey in North America until English colonization. It is said that the eastern American Indians considered the appearance of the honeybee among them to be a harbinger of white encroachment. It meant that the white man was less than seventy-five miles away and that it was time to move westward to safer territory.

❖ ❖ ❖

Even at Bent's Fort, they ate chicken. Throughout New Mexico, fowls were on the menu. Inexpensive, quickly reproducing, and a source for egg money, chickens were raised by nearly everyone. Even today, in Santa Fe, chickens are raised within the city limits, and *el gallo tuerto*, the old cockeyed rooster (a common Hispanic name for crowing roosters), cries out his hymn to the sun every morning. Here's a traditional and scrumptious stewed hen recipe from New Mexico:

Stewed Hen in Red Chile

Cut up the chicken and boil 15 minutes. Add two chopped onions, several cloves of garlic, two bay leaves, oregano, a pinch of thyme, and salt to taste. Allow to simmer, covered, until nearly done, then add two to three dried, crumbled, large red chile pods. The more seeds you leave in, the hotter the stew will be. Add one cup of ripe olives, two cups dry sherry, and continue cooking, uncovered. Three tablespoons of cornstarch mixed with cold water may be then added to the gravy. Simmer another 5 minutes and serve over rice. (Recipe collection of Sam Arnold.)

Susan Magoffin Discovers New Mexican Delights

Eight months after crossing the Santa Fe Trail, on February 15, 1847, Susan Magoffin, the teenaged bride from Kentucky, reached El Paso del Norte. There, she awaited word on the fate of the American troops fighting just ahead in Chihuahua. The Magoffins, Susan and her husband Samuel, stayed for two days in the house of an affluent native-born "Spaniard." Noted Susan:

> Our dishes are all Mexican, but good ones, some are delightful; one great importance, they are well cooked; their meats are all boiled, the healthiest way of preparing them, and are in most instances cooked with vegetables, which are onions, cabbage and tomatoes; with the addition of apples and grapes; the courses for dinner are four, one dish at a time; for breakfast two, ending always with beans. Brandy and wine are regularly put on at each meal, and never go off without being honored with the salutations of all the company (Magoffin, 206).

Trimming Chicken

Susan Magoffin also favorably reports eating *sopa de arroz*, a traditional early New Mexican dish of rice and eggs. Here is the recipe:

Sopa de Arroz

Fry the bacon, oil, onion, and garlic together until bacon is browned and onions are well cooked. Add the rice and stir into the hot, oily, onion-bacon mix, coating the rice as much as possible by mixing well with a spoon. The rice will not appear coated, but the oil will touch each grain.

Add chicken bouillon and bring the whole to a boil. Simmer 10 minutes. Then, cook tightly covered on lowest heat available until rice is done (about 15 more minutes). Serve garnished with egg halves, a little parsley or cilantro, and some bits of red chile or sweet red pepper for color. Chopped tomatoes are sometimes added to this dish in the beginning stages of cooking, although their inclusion is not historically precedented. (Recipe collection of Sam Arnold.)

2 cups rice
4 cups chicken bouillon
3 tablespoons oil
1 onion, minced
2 garlic cloves, minced
4 strips bacon, finely minced
boiled eggs
parsley or cilantro
red chile or sweet red
    pepper, chopped fine

In Mora, New Mexico, where Ceran St. Vrain ran a flour mill and is buried, there is an old but wonderfully good recipe for a New Mexican stuffed chicken from the Santa Fe Trail period:

Pollo Relleno

In a large pot, simmer the beef 1 hour in beef bouillon until well done. Mince beef fine and make a stuffing by adding the golden sultana raisins, minced onion, cloves, cinnamon, salt, chile and chimajá. Boil chicken in some chicken broth for approximately 12 minutes. Brown the stuffing in three tablespoons of oil or lard, then stuff it in the chicken cavity. Bake the chicken at 350º F. for approximately 35 minutes or until it is tender, basting with the meat stock. (Recipe collection of Sam Arnold.)

1 large fryer chicken
1 pound round steak
1 quart beef broth
¾ cup golden sultana raisins
1 small onion, minced
½ teaspoon cinnamon
1 pinch cloves
½ teaspoon salt
1 teaspoon chimajá
1 tablespoon red chile caribe
oil or lard

Susan Magoffin cared little for her first introduction to New Mexico cheeses: "Their cheese is clabber and made on the same principle as the Dutch smerecase though very tough, mean looking, and to me, unpalatable. Oh, how my heart sickened to say nothing of my stomach . . . a cheese . . . the kind we saw yesterday from the Mora . . . entirely speckled over" (Magoffin, 90, 94).

Corn and Bean Soup (a hearty soup, eaten by Susan Magoffin in 1846)

1 pint fresh corn, cut from
    ears, canned, or frozen
1 pint pinto beans
2 quarts cold water
1 onion, sliced
1 large clove garlic
1 cup red chile puree
1 tablespoon oregano
pinch cumin
2 teaspoons salt

Soak beans overnight in cold water, then slowly boil for most of the day until soft. Add corn and other ingredients, reserving salt till last. When you need to add water to the cooking beans, add hot water; putting cold water onto cooking beans toughens them. Serve the bean-and-corn soup with some grated goat's milk cheese or Monterey Jack. Fried croutons add a nice touch. (Recipe collection of Sam Arnold.)

Garbanzos

Garbanzos, also known as chick-peas, have been a staple of New Mexican dishes for generations, although they are not as popular as they used to be. These mealy little nuggets are easy to grow, and can be cooked in combination with other dishes or served by themselves in the following recipe:

Garbanzos with Chile

1 cup dry garbanzos
1 onion, chopped
½ cup red chile puree
a few sprigs of cilantro
salt to taste
water
bacon fat or salt pork

Soak garbanzos overnight in a pot of water. Bring pot to a boil, drain, and cover garbanzos with fresh heated water. Do not add cold water, as this will toughen them. Add salt and cilantro, then continue to boil for perhaps 2 hours, until soft.

Meanwhile, fry onion in one spoonful of bacon fat or with some salt pork. Drain the garbanzos and toss them into the pan with the cooked onion. Add chile and reheat just before serving. If at all possible, avoid using canned garbanzos. (Recipe collection of Sam Arnold.)

Hot Chocolate

Breakfast time in El Paso was described by Susan Magoffin as follows: "We have chocolate every morning on rising, breakfast about 10 o'k [sic], dinner at two, chocolate again at dark, and supper at 9 o'clock" (Magoffin, 208). Here's a rich, delicious recipe:

Mexican Chocolate (four cups)

Boil grated chocolate in water and cook for a few minutes. Add other ingredients and cook slowly in a double boiler, beating hard frequently until thick and foamy. Do not overheat, as egg will solidify. (The cinnamon and the egg, along with prolonged beating, are the great secrets of Mexican chocolate.) (Recipe collection of Sam Arnold.)

2 squares sweet dark chocolate, grated
1 cup cream
½ cup boiling water
salt to taste
2 cups milk
4 tablespoons sugar
dash nutmeg
1 egg
1 teaspoon vanilla
2 teaspoons cinnamon

Mexican Chocolate, Short Version

Heat as many cups of milk as you wish to serve. Place in blender with one square Mexican chocolate and one egg yolk per cup of milk. Blend at slow speed to prevent hot milk from jumping out. Gradually increase blender speed until mixture is frothy. Serve at once. (Recipe collection of Sam Arnold.)

In Yucatan, they still make chocolate from the original Mayan recipe. They simply boil one tablet of Mexican chocolate (chocolate, sugar, and cinnamon) in one cup of water for about 5 minutes to extract the flavor from the beans. Then, the mixture is beaten until frothy and served. It's quite different from the milk mixture, and, quite possibly, American adults would prefer it. It has a water-based taste, rather like some of the instant coffees with chocolate now on the market.

In southern Mexico, women still buy cacao beans, sugar, and almonds. At the store, the cacao and almonds are poured into a grinding machine, which extrudes a satin-smooth, sticky chocolate. As it emerges, this chocolate is sprinkled with sugar to keep it from sticking to the container below. It is ground a second time with a large quantity of sugar, then taken home, molded into small tablets, and dried for later.

Tablets or slabs of chocolate have been cherished by New Mexican chocolate fanciers for nearly four centuries. In probate inventories, slabs of chocolate were listed among the estate assets of New Mexicans as early as the seventeenth century. Shortly after the Spanish invasion of Mexico in the early sixteenth century, Fray Bernardino de Sahagún listed orange, black, and white chocolate, sometimes mixed with sweetening or purple flowers, in his book *General History of the Things of New Spain*. He indicated that chocolate was a beverage primarily of the nobleman or rich merchant (Sahagún, 37–40). It was believed to have a hallucinogenic effect, rather like the magic mushrooms, and was considered an aphrodisiac. Chocolate gained its reputation as an aphrodisiac in Europe, where there were laws governing its consumption in Austria.

The Market

Going to market was a daily ritual for the servants of the *ricos*. Often, these marketing expeditions provided the main source of social interaction for New Mexican women. Here's a description of a typical mid-nineteenth-century New Mexican market:

> The markets have . . . great quantities of "Chile Colorado" and "verde," "cebollas" or onions, "sandias" or watermelons, "huevos" or eggs, "queso" or cheese, and "hojas" or corn husks, neatly tied up in bundles for making the cigarritos, "punche" or tobacco, "uvas" or grapes, and "pinones," nuts of the pine tree, (pinus monophyllus). These last are slightly

Indian Corn

baked to make them keep, and are brought to market in great quantities. Besides these things, there are many varieties of bread, and several kinds of meat. The Pueblo Indians bring in great quantities of peaches which are here called "duraznos" (*Abert's New Mexico Report*, 46).

Bread was also available from vendors in the plaza, and Lieutenant Abert made these notes in Santa Fe in the summer of 1846: "I understand that the flour is sifted by hand, and, instead of yeast, they use the dough from the previous day's mixing. One kind of flour is quite coarse and dark; this sells in Taos for $2.50 the fanega (144 pounds)" (*Abert's New Mexico Report*, 57).

Santa Fe Newspaper Ads

By 1846, after more than a quarter century of trade with the United States, Santa Fe boasted well-filled stores stocked with a wide variety of merchandise. Susan Magoffin's description of supping on "cold champaign [sic] and oysters" in July 1846, indicates the sophistication of foodstuffs available (Magoffin, 105).

In 1847, the *Santa Fe Republican* ran ads from the St. Vrain & Bent Company (the firm's name was changed, possibly after the death of Charles Bent) listing coffee, sugar, molasses, oysters, mackerel, cheese, candies, saleratus, raisins, bacon, ham, and bottle champaign (*sic*), sardines, sperm candles, tobacco, and cigars. Other firms listed barrels of Ohio whiskey, brandy, gin, loaf sugar, peach brandy, Stoughton's bitters, essence of lemon and orange, and peppermint.

Isleta Pueblo

Famed frontiersman Francis X. Aubry ran an ad on November 11, 1847, offering gin, brandy and port wines for sale. One of the "champaigns" offered was "Silleraeux [sic] Mosseaux." Several ads tout "El Passo [sic] wines," which are listed as "equal to any in Santa Fe." In the *Republican*, September 17, 1847, a story notes that "wine for home consumption was being produced at all the ranchos up to Santa Fe." Benjamin F. Coon's store also ran an ad on October 1, 1847, listing French and American brandy, old rye whiskey, New England rum, Holland gin, old Madeira, port wines, and claret and brandy cherries by the box.

New Mexican Cuisine

At the time of the Santa Fe Trail, from 1821 to 1870, the foods of the generally peaceful agricultural Pueblo Indians were introduced to Americans. The Hispanic population, made up heavily of descendants of Tlaxcalan Indians from Mexico and of the few *hidalgos*, native-born Spaniards, had its cuisines, and the mixture homogenized into what is now called New Mexican cuisine.

Corn Tortillas

As explained in Chapter 1, the "Mexican flavor" of corn tortillas comes from the lime (calcium hydroxide) flavor that remains after the corn kernel has lost its hull and been washed several times. During the boiling process, the kernels become partially cooked. Stirring releases the hard hulls, which float to the surface and are scooped off. The corn is then dried for later use or ground into a meal (masa harina) or paste. Tortillas are made from this dried, ground hominy corn that has been moistened with water to form a paste. The paste is immediately shaped into very thin, round discs that are placed on a flat sheet-iron or clay baking surface called a *comal* to bake. Tortillas may be eaten plain, used flat or rolled for enchiladas, fried as taco shells, or cut in wedge-shaped pieces for tortilla chips. A little salt on the comal keeps them from sticking.

Piki

Although corn tortillas were the basic "bread" of the New Mexicans, some Pueblo Indians also prepared *piki*, also called guayave:

They brought out circular baskets, nearly flat, these were filled with a kind of corn bread or "guayave" [Spanish for guava]. It bears a striking resemblance to a hornet's nest; it is of the same color, and it is as thin as a wafer. The "guayave" they crumbled up between their fingers and put into a second basket from which we ate (*Abert's New Mexico Report,* 87).

To make piki, or guayave, ground blue cornmeal mixed with sage ashes, water, and salt to form a gruel is smeared on a hot rock griddle by hand, then quickly rolled. In *Commerce of the Prairies,* Josiah Gregg also speaks of *guayabes* at Taos pueblo (Gregg, 149).

Tamales

The corn paste used to make tortillas may also be mixed with fat to make tamales. If any one dish speaks of New Mexico, it's a plate of pork or chicken meat hot tamales topped with a red chile sauce. This Mexican dish, dating back years before the voyages of Columbus, consists of a smear of fat-enriched nixtamal paste spread on a corn husk or two (one is often not wide enough). A blob of filling of some sort is then spread on the corn (nixtamal)-and-lard paste. Longwise, the husks spread with paste and filling are folded over, rolled, sealed and then steamed. When properly prepared and steamed, the corn mash becomes light and rather fluffy and makes a firm, thickened covering for the inner filling. Various fillings are used: chopped meat with red chile puree; a piccata type of sweetened mince-meat with pine nuts and raisins; freshly-grated corn; chicken; beef; pork; and, among the Pueblo Indians, a red-chile-flavored bean filling.

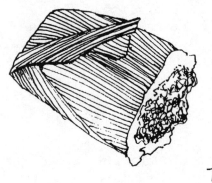

Tamale

Tamale Ingredients:

48 or more dried corn husks soaked in hot water for one-half hour or longer

⅓ cup lard (other shortenings may be used, but lard is best)

2 cups *masa harina* (a hominy-corn flour commercially made by the Quaker Oats Company, among others)

2 teaspoons baking powder

2 teaspoons salt

1-½ cups chicken stock

Mix well and cool in refrigerator

Tamale Filling:

4 cups chopped meat (cooked pork, beef, chicken, goat, or lamb)

1 cup minced onion

1 cup red chile puree

pinch of oregano

1 teaspoon garlic salt (or fry meat with fresh garlic and onions)

½ cup cooked pinto beans (optional)

Recipe for Tamales (yields 24)

Make a tasty mixture of the meat and chile, adding perhaps one-half cup cooked pinto beans. The fillings can be as widely varied as your imagination allows. Kernel corn and toasted piñon nuts with a little red chile makes an excellent vegetarian filling. Minced cooked pork with toasted walnut pieces, raisins, and onions is a delicious variation. Fresh, green corn kernels and grated cheese worked into the masa is also wonderful with just a smear of red chile puree.

Smooth out about three tablespoons of the masa (dough) and spread it evenly, about five inches long by four inches wide, almost to the sides, in the middle of two pre-soaked corn husks overlapping end to end. Next, drop a heaping tablespoon or more of the meat filling in the center of the dough and spread evenly over the masa. Roll the corn husk lengthwise into a cylinder. The traditionalist folds the ends back over, then ties off the tamale's two ends with strings of split corn husk. Trim off the corn husk ends neatly to make an attractive "sausage" of the corn husk and filling. Lay the tamales vertically in a large colander and steam for 1 hour. (Recipe collection of Sam Arnold.)

Many fascinating varieties of tamales were found in Montezuma's court at the time of the Spanish Conquest. Among them were "tamales made of maize flowers with ground amaranth seed and cherries added . . . tamales stuffed with amaranth greens . . . tamales made with honey . . . white tamales with maize grains thrown in . . . tamales of meat cooked with maize and yellow chile; roast turkey hen and roast quail (Sahagún, 37–38).

Hominy Corn (Posole)

One of the most basic New World foods is hominy corn, ground or dried for later use. The skinless corn kernels were often boiled in fresh water to make a dish called *posole*, sometimes spelled *pozole*. When cooked for 4 to 5 hours, each hominy kernel swells up and pops, resembling solid popcorn. Posole is the name for both the hull-less grains of hominy corn and the popular dish.

Posole, or hominy corn, was a basic Indian dish prepared throughout the Americas wherever corn grew. The first New England colonists found the local Narragansett Indians eating samp — their version of hominy. It was not long before hominy corn was adopted throughout the colonies. It is still a common dish in the south.

In New Mexico, posole is both prepared and served in a fairly simple manner. Santa Fe Trail travelers soon knew it well. Here are some of the old recipes they enjoyed:

Posole
(Hog and Hominy)

Fry onions in fat, add pork, and brown. Deglaze pan, adding all to a deep pot with white posole, chicken broth, chile, and seasonings (a few chicken pieces add extra flavor). Simmer for 5 to 6 hours, until pork is thoroughly tender and posole has popped. Use either damp or dry white posole corn. Yellow posole is not as good, and canned hominy is a travesty. Serves six. (Recipe collection of Sam Arnold.)

2 pounds pork shoulder, cubed
4 quarts chicken broth
2 onions, chopped
1 bay leaf
1 tablespoon fat
½ teaspoon oregano
1 cup red chile pulp or 4 to 6 tablespoons pure New Mexico red chile powder
2 cups wet or dry white posole corn (hominy); if dry, soak overnight
2 teaspoons salt

Posole with Pork and Green Chile

Roast and peel eighteen fresh chiles. Chop them and add to the posole as prepared in the above recipe, substituting them for the red chile powder or pulp. Serve in large bowls with hot, buttered corn tortillas. (To heat tortillas easily, sprinkle a little salt on your frying pan or griddle. It will elevate the tortillas slightly above the heat, allowing easy turning and less burning.) (Recipe collection of Sam Arnold).

6 pig's feet
2 quarts chicken broth
1 onion, chopped
2 cloves garlic, chopped
1 tablespoon fat
1 teaspoon Mexican leaf
    oregano
½ cup red chile pulp or 4 to
    6 tablespoons chile pow-
    der
1 teaspoon salt
3 cups white posole corn

Trotter Posole

Tie pig's feet in a cheesecloth bag and cook in broth until tender. Brown onion and garlic in fat and add to the broth and pig's feet. Then add chile, oregano, salt, and hominy. Simmer in broth slowly about 5 hours, or until hominy is cooked. Remove the trotter bag, strip meat from bones, chop meat, and return to pot. Serves six to eight. (Recipe collection of Sam Arnold.)

Further south in Mexico, posole becomes more complex. It's included in various types of dishes; in one recipe, the corn is cooked with pieces of chicken. At the table, a soup dish is served, containing rich chicken broth, chicken pieces, and just a few pieces of hominy corn. Small bowls of shredded lettuce, shredded radishes, ground red chiles, fried crisp, black muleta chiles, minced fresh tomato, and minced fresh onion are set out on the table, and the diner adds as much as he likes of these items to the basic chicken-and-hominy-corn soup.

Chiles

On encountering her first chile-pepper-hot meal in New Mexico, Susan Magoffin, the observant young bride of Samuel Magoffin, American trader and agent, wrote in her 1846 diary:

and then the dinner . . . half a dozen tortillas made of blue corn, and not a plate, but [w]rapped in a napkin, twin brother to the last tablecloth . . . so black with dirt and gre[a]se that it resembled more the common brown rather than the white sheeting of which it was really made. . . . Oh, how my heart sickened to say nothing of my stomach, a

> cheese and the kind we saw yesterday from the mora entirely
> speckled over and 2 earthern jollas (ollas-jars) of a mixture
> of meat, chilly verde [green chile] & onions boiled together
> completing course No. 1. . . . [T]here were a few mouthfuls
> taken, for I could not eat a dish so strong, and unaccustumed
> to my palate (Magoffin, 94).

This was Susan's introduction to the chile culture of New Mexico. Later, however, she would develop an affection for the food and even wrote in her diary of "preparing a cookery book" so that her friends in the "States" could enjoy the new tastes she had discovered.

Chile, botanically termed "capsicum," is a pepper indigenous to the Americas, according to ethno-botanists. One of the treasures Columbus brought back to Spain on his second voyage was a quantity of chile seeds. Later Spanish and Portuguese explorers spread chile seeds around the world. Chile is erroneously believed to have been named for the country on the west coast of South America. Actually, the term derives from the Aztec names for various peppers — *quauchilli, milchilee, zenalchilli,* and others.

Chiles come in many varieties, from the tiny, round, raisin chiles to the huge, pointed pods called Big Jims. There are the small, pointed ones (*chiles serranos*), the short, stubby, fat ones (*jalapeños*), and the very long, narrow Italian variety, some light red or orange when ripe, others virtually black. On the Ivory Coast of Africa, one finds the tiny, immensely hot *pili-pili* pepper, and in Mexico, the *habanero,* a plump, baby-tomato-shaped, light yellow-green chile found primarily in Yucatan. The habanero is so hot that most people handle it with gloves on and only rub a cut piece of the pepper across the item to be flavored. Its chile oil is so potent that it blisters skin upon contact. In Jamaica, it's known as "scotch bonnet." Dr. Antonio Morino, a Mexican chile authority, claims roughly 200 different types of chiles in existence with over 100 varieties in Mexico alone.

Chile fans know that almost any pepper, if left on the plant until the end of the season, will change from green to red. *Chile verde* (green chile) is simply picked earlier. Green chile is

Serrano Chilies

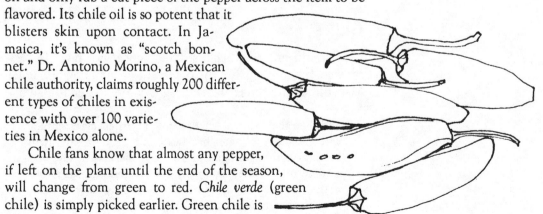

not necessarily hotter than red chile; hotness of flavor depends upon the pod, the plant, the type of chile, the soil, and the growing conditions. The seeds are often hotter than the pod flesh. Inside the chile, near the stem, a little blister of chile oil, called capsaicin, forms within a fine membrane. Until that blister is broken and the hot oil spills out within the pepper, every chile is as bland as an English bell pepper. The oil sack may be broken when the chile is bumped, picked, or packed; even the wind blowing one chile against another can cause the oil sack to rupture. Since the seeds are nearest to the sack, they absorb most of the chile oil. So, by removing the seeds and the long stringers inside the chile, one may diminish the hotness, if desired.

The chile purist does not buy ground chile powder, even "pure ground New Mexican chile," because the producers do not usually remove the stems and seeds from the dried pods before grinding. Instead, they throw the whole chile, stem and all, good pods and the not so good, together into the grinder. The result is a chile that is hotter and not nearly as good as homemade, prepared with dried red pods.

Basic Red Chile Puree

Roast 6 to 8 dried red chile pods in a hot (400º F.) oven for 5 minutes to enhance flavor (some people prefer not to toast them). Wash the chiles and break off the stems. While rinsing under cold water, run your finger inside the dried pod, opening it to look for moldy areas and to loosen seeds for the water to wash away. New Mexicans leave some seeds, claiming they give "life" to the chile. Put the seed-free pods into a blender with three-quarters cup of hot water, one small garlic clove (if you like), a dash of salt, and one-half teaspoon of leaf oregano. Blend at high speed for approximately 1 minute to make a puree. (Recipe collection of Sam Arnold.)

Red chile puree may be used in many ways. For example, add it to a flour-and-oil roux, cook, and then add broth to make an enchilada sauce. Or heat it and pour over breakfast eggs; add to soups or to chopped meat to make chile con carne. The purist does not add onions, beans, or tomatoes (tomato adds an acid flavor which overrides the delicacy of the chile pod and frequently makes it much more difficult to digest).

It is a mistake to believe that eating chile is hard on the digestion. Indigestion following a Mexican meal often results from too much oil and the use of acidic tomato in the preparation. Using the pod itself with lean meat will result in a tasty, low-fat combination of flavors that is easy to digest and provides a marvelous sense of well-being after eating.

Although other countries in the Americas love chiles, only Mexico and Guatemala have a highly developed chile-eating culture. Ward's *Mexico* describes a market in Zacatecas, in 1820: "The quantity of Chile disposed of was really prodigious; waggons laden with it, drawn each by six oxen, were arriving hourly from Aguas Calientes, yet their contents rapidly disappeared, piles of Capsicum sufficient to excoriate the palates of half London vanishing in the course of a few minutes" (Ward, 611).

Green chile (the long green Anaheim-type chile) may be found fresh, dried, in cans, or frozen. The pods are picked while green, usually cleaned, and if not processed immediately to remove the skins, often hung to dry in the sun. Commercial firms may dip them in a bath of alkali, or they may be roasted over hot fires to blister and loosen the skins.

Many people add tomatoes to their green chile and meat in order to lessen the burn. Many restaurants, seeking "hotter" green chile, simply chop up the short, stubby jalapeño to give the fire to a version of chile verde. Both these practices are reprehensible to the chile purist.

Grinding Corn

Chile con Carne
(New Mexico village-style "red" or "green")

4 pounds moderately lean
    pork shoulder
3 quarts water
4 tablespoons oil (lard in the
    old days)
4 tablespoons flour
1 teaspoon salt
1 cup basic red chile puree
    or 2 cups chopped green
    chile pods
1 teaspoon beef bouillon
    concentrate
2 garlic cloves, smashed

Boil pork for 1 hour. Remove, retaining broth, then chop into medium-sized pieces. In a frying pan, brown pork pieces in oil and add garlic, more oil, and flour after meat is seared. Push meat to side, stir flour, oil, and garlic mixture to a roux, and cook for 1 minute, or until bubbling. Then, add beef-bouillon concentrate mixed with some of the broth. Remove all back to pot of broth and deglaze the pan. Add red chile puree or green chile, oregano, and salt, if desired.

If green chile is used, there should be nearly as much green chile as meat. If beef is used instead of pork, cut steak pieces into small three-quarter-inch cubes, or have your butcher run chuck through the chile plate of his meat grinder twice. Either is preferable to the squished, extruded hamburger sold in supermarkets. Some people prefer to omit the oil-flour roux and simply add a little masa harina or blue cornmeal (about two tablespoonsful), which thickens the chile somewhat and gives a good flavor. (Remember to stir your meal into cold water first before adding it to the pot.) (Recipe collection of Sam Arnold.)

Carne Adobada

Using a red chile puree, thoroughly coat raw pork slices or cutlets arranged on a tray. Allow meat to marinate in the refrigerator for at least 1 day (preferably 3). Roast in a 350º F. oven until brown. If chile begins to burn, lower the heat. If the pork has sufficient fat, it will baste the meat, keeping it crisp. Hardly anything tastes better. (Recipe collection of Sam Arnold.)

Dicho (a saying)

"A la primera cocinera se le va un chile entero" (to the best lady cook goes a whole chile), is an old, humorous Mexican phrase. Surely no kitchen can be without either.

The Best Chile?

The best red chiles in America (according to most chile connoisseurs) come from the area north of Española, New Mexico. The chiles grown there seem to have a richness of flavor and a piquancy that is beloved by the chile lover. Chile is a matter of local pride, with the villages of Dixon, Truchas, Trampas, Chimayo, and others each claiming the crown. The Indian pueblos also grow chiles, and each variety has its advocates. Other New Mexican chiles from Hatch, Socorro, Las Lunas, Santa Rosa, and Las Cruces also have their proponents. Northern New Mexicans say that the Hatch chiles, most often the ones brought north to be sold in the Española area, are sweet, pungent pods, but do not have quite the subtlety of flavor found in the locally grown chile.

The Española valley chile has a shorter pod, is puckered up, and makes a reddish-orange puree. The experienced eye can spot the difference, though it's difficult to describe. If you know your New Mexican purveyor, you can sometimes buy the better local chiles, which are kept primarily for local use. They may charge double, but the taste is superb.

Until the evolution of the blender, the method of reconstituting dried red chile pods was to soak and boil them, then put them through a fine sieve or food mill. Today, virtually every Spanish-speaking home where chile is eaten has a blender. It is a simple matter to tear off a half-dozen pods and make the puree previously described.

Chile also has long been considered a medicinal plant. In a medicinal compilation published in Rome in 1651, there were at least seven varieties of chile recognized by the Aztecs as having medicinal value (Curtin, 62). They were employed variously as remedies for kidney and brain inflammation, lung problems, heart pains, "bad blood," diarrhea, and internal tumors. The Mayans also prepared chile remedies. Red chile was mixed with salt and put outside into the dew until dawn, then drunk to cure blood in the stools. Ground red chile mixed with honey and tobacco leaf was boiled, and the tea sipped alternately with cold water as a remedy for an irritated throat.

To grow chiles in New Mexico, seeds were planted in March and April in whatever tins and boxes were available. The seeds were allowed to germinate on the broad window ledges. May 3 was considered the last day upon which the young shoots could be transplanted to open gardens. By early September, healthy green chile pods were growing on the plants, and by mid- or late September, they had turned scarlet and were ready for picking and stringing.

In southern Colorado and New Mexico there has always been considerable belief in witchcraft (*brujería*). According to folk tradition, one may burn a witch's spells by tying two large nails in the shape of a cross with a piece of wire. The cross is heated red-hot in a fire, and chile pods and whole, Mexican rock salt are placed upon it. The rock salt, to which a little kerosene has been added, should be sprinkled with a motion describing the cross. The resulting flame is supposed to burn away any spells (Curtin, 64).

Desserts

Desserts were enjoyed by the country folk. Rice was cheap and was eaten extensively by New Mexicans. Rice pudding, consequently, was a favorite village dessert.

Arroz Dulce
(New Mexican Rice Pudding)

5 cups milk
1 cup rice
salt to taste
1 large can evaporated milk
1 cup sugar
2 teaspoons vanilla

Scald the milk and evaporated milk, then put the rice into a deep baking dish. Pour the milk mixture over the top and bake in a 300º F. oven for 3 hours or until rice is just done. Sometimes the heavy uncooked grains fall to the bottom of the dish, so stir these from time to time during the first hour. Add the vanilla, sugar, and salt when the rice has reached the al dente stage. Mix in and bake for another half hour. (Recipe collection of Sam Arnold.)

Cajeta

Another delicious, traditional dessert is *cajeta*, a cooked goat's milk, caramel syrup. It is a thick sauce made of milk and sugar that has been cooked a long time at a low temperature until the sugar caramelizes. Cajeta tastes a bit like butterscotch sauce. It is sometimes eaten with crackers, and sometimes a small spoonful sprinkled with a few toasted peanuts is served on a dessert plate. The term "cajeta" originated in Mexico. Originally, it was the name for the small wooden boxes used to store candies and fruits. Later, it was applied to the sweet dessert. The Mexican town of Selaya has developed a large cajeta industry known throughout Latin America. If you can obtain goat's milk, here is the recipe:

Cajeta de Leche

Put the cow's and goat's milk into a saucepan and bring to a boil. Mix the cornstarch, soda, and one-half cup cow's milk together and stir the mixture into the boiling milk. Stir the sugar gradually into the milk. Continue boiling the mixture until it is just beginning to thicken — about 40 to 50 minutes, depending on the depth of the cajeta in the pan. Then, continue to cook, stirring constantly, until cajeta coats the back of a spoon and forms a thread when spoon is lifted. Pour the cajeta into a dish to cool before serving. From start to finish, cajeta will take approximately 1-½ hours to cook. (Recipe collection of Sam Arnold.)

1 quart goat's milk
3 cups cow's milk
¾ teaspoon cornstarch
¼ scant teaspoon baking soda
½ cup cow's milk
1-½ cups granulated sugar
½ cup granulated sugar

An easy shortcut that does not produce quite the same taste but is a reasonable substitute follows:

Eagle Brand Cajeta

Place one unopened can of Eagle brand sweetened condensed milk in a pot of boiling water. Cook for 4 hours. The milk will become somewhat golden, as the sugar within it tends to caramelize. Use as is. The company may discourage you from boiling an unopened can, though I've never known one to explode. Be careful; perhaps cover with a lid and keep at low boiling heat. (Recipe collection of Sam Arnold.)

New Mexico Goat's Milk Cheese

1 gallon fresh goat's milk
1 rennet (junket) tablet

Crush the tablet to powder and add to lukewarm (baby-bottle temperature) milk. After a solid clabber forms — perhaps 30 minutes — stir and place in a cheesecloth bag. Hang bag over a large pan to collect the draining whey. Mold the curds into a cake and serve with brown-sugar syrup and cream. A variation is to slice it, sprinkle with brown sugar, and place briefly under a broiler to caramelize the sugar. (Recipe collection of Sam Arnold.)

Requesones
(cheese from whey)

Slowly boil whey with your pan only half on the heat source so that the boil comes up slowly from one side. One-half cup at a time, pour in sweet milk until you have a mixture of equal parts milk and whey. This will form a curd, which you can dip out using a cheesecloth-covered strainer. It is a very delicate curd cheese that may be served as is or with brown sugar sprinkled lightly over the curds. (This recipe is partly my own; part is taken from Erna Ferguson's Mexican Cookbook, 104.)

Capirotada

A dessert mentioned by many travelers along the Mexican part of the Santa Fe Trail was *capirotada*, a bread pudding made with brown sugar, cheese, onions, raisins, and spices. Dating back at least to medieval days, capirotada is a Friday Lenten dish and one of the things that makes the Season of Sorrow a pleasant time in Mexico. Food historian Charles Perry says that his researches indicate that capirotada descends from a favorite dish of the seventh-century prophet Mohammed.

Diego Granado's cookbook *Libro del Arte Cozina*, published in 1599, lists three capirotada recipes. They are entrees using baked layers of toasted bread, onion, and cheese, as the main capirotada theme. To these are added layers of meat, quail, or partridge, wine, and a topping of sweet meringue. From this unusual recipe has evolved today's capirotada, or sopa, as it's now called in New Mexico. Onions in a dessert may seem strange, but when cooked, they add a pleasing, apple-like flavor and texture. (And they give the food historian a link to the distant past.)

Recipe for Capirotada, or Spotted Dog

Boil the sugar and water to make a syrup approximately the consistency of maple syrup. When syrup has thickened slightly, add the onion pieces, letting them cook together. In a bowl, stir eggs and milk together. Don't beat! In a large baking dish, layer broken bread, then syrup, raisins, apples, onions, butter, cinnamon, and nutmeg until dish is filled. Bake approximately 45 minutes at 350º F. After 40 minutes, remove from oven and spread cheese over the top. Replace in oven for 5 minutes, or until cheese is melted. Serve hot. Pour a little cold heavy cream over each portion. Serves eight hungry people. (The grizzled American mountain men sometimes had difficulty with Spanish words. Because of the raisins in this bread pudding, it was affectionately dubbed "spotted dog" by the early westerners.)

6 cups toasted bread pieces
2 cups crushed piloncillo or
   brown sugar
1 cup water in a small pan
1 medium-sized onion,
   chopped in small pieces
4 eggs
2 cups sliced apples
3 cups milk
1 cup sultana raisins
½ pound butter or margarine
2 tablespoons cinnamon
1 teaspoon nutmeg
1 cup grated yellow cheddar-
   style cheese
heavy cream

Budin de Garbanzo

2 cups dry garbanzos
water to cover
pinch salt
2 tablespoons flour
6 egg yolks, beaten
6 egg whites, beaten stiff
1 cup dark brown sugar or 2
    large melted piloncillos
2 tablespoons butter
leaves from 6 sprigs fresh ci-
    lantro

Garbanzos can also be used to make a delicious dessert with a mealy, nut-like flavor: Soak dry garbanzos in water overnight. Boil garbanzos about 3 hours, and then, when soft, mash them with a potato ricer or puree in food processor. Stir in the flour, beaten egg yolks, cilantro, and a little salt. Beat the egg whites stiff and fold these into the garbanzo mixture. Place mixture in a buttered and flour-dusted baking dish with a few lumps of butter left on the bottom. Mix in brown sugar, cover dish with lid or foil, place in water bath (simply a larger pot filled with water in which you put the pudding baking dish), and bake for 1-½ hours at 350º F. You will be surprised at how delicious this dish is. (Recipe collection of Sam Arnold.)

Piñon Nuts

Gathered by Hispanics and Indians in New Mexico, pine nuts are the fruit of the piñon tree, a Spanish scrub pine found throughout the West, whose wood, when burned, emits an incense-like smoke. The nuts, collected in the fall, are prized for their flavor, as many nineteenth-century travelers along the Santa Fe Trail noted.

In *Commerce of the Prairies*, Josiah Gregg cites a journal entry from the 1820s recording a wagon train en route to Missouri that carried two gallons of pine-nut oil. He notes that the "delicate, sweet flavor generated when these nuts are roasted would make it a serious rival to sesame oil" (Gregg, 81). Lieutenant Abert, too, praised the pine nut, calling it "exceedingly pleasant to the taste," and noted that according to Gregg, "considerable quantities are exported annually to the southern cities and . . . they are sometimes used for the manufacture of oil which may be used as a substitute for lamp oil [as a source of lamplight, piñon oil was less noisome than tallow or whale oil and less volatile than the explosive combination of alcohol and turpentine]. They form the chief article of food of the Pueblos and New Mexicans" (Abert, 14).

After the piñon nuts are collected, they are roasted and eaten. Before the invention of the hulling machine, the hard, paper-thin shells of the roasted *piñones* were cracked between the teeth, the meat extracted, and the hulls expelled from the mouth. The nuts are still quite popular in Santa Fe (moviegoers tread on a crackling carpet of piñon-nut shells at local theaters). Man, however, is not the only New Mexican fancier of pine nuts. Large caches of piñones are sometimes found after snowstorms by following the tracks of ground squirrels, who hide as much as twenty pounds of nuts per burrow.

Sheep Ranching

Though not without its drawbacks, sheep ranching was a lucrative business in New Mexico: "The raising of sheep would be much more profitable if it were not for the depredations of the Navajos. Even now, great numbers are raised, whose flesh is as fine as any I have ever tasted. Some of the ricos on the Rio del Norte are said to own 40,000 sheep" (*Abert's New Mexico Report*, 52).

Nothing tastes better than a good Indian lamb stew. Traditionally, Navajos don't use any chile, but many of the young people have succumbed, like the rest of us, to a chile addiction. Here's a traditional New Mexican village stew using lamb or mutton:

1 whole lamb shoulder, cut in fist-sized pieces
4 onions, coarsely chopped
2 whole garlic heads, with cloves peeled and split lengthwise
½ cup flour
¼ cup cooking oil
4 quarts stock from boiling browned lamb bones
6 peeled potatoes, cut in bite-sized cubes
2 red peppers
2 cups cubed summer squash
2 cups young green corn, cut fresh from cobs
6 peaches, stoned and cut in cubes
1 cup celery tops, chopped
6 juniper berries
¼ cup mint leaves
¼ cup cilantro leaves

Caldo de Cordero (serves twelve)

In a deep pot, heat oil until it begins to smoke. Quickly add the onions and garlic. Next, add lamb pieces rolled in flour and brown all. Add stock and potatoes. Cook slowly for 1 hour, adding broth if needed to keep meat covered. Then, add the rest of the ingredients: pepper, corn, squash, peaches, celery, juniper, mint, and cilantro. Cook for 5 minutes more and serve. (Recipe collection of Sam Arnold.)

New Mexican Breakfast

In his *New Mexico Report*, Lieutenant Abert describes a Mexican breakfast served near Santo Domingo: "He gave us 'los entranos de carnero' [guts], and tripe chopped up; also an abundance of tortillas and milk that had been salted and boiled. The milk is prepared thus in order to keep it during warm weather from turning sour. One big goblet of water was set in the middle of the table. From this, we were all to drink" (*Abert's New Mexico Report*, 66).

Wealthy Households

Lieutenant Abert also describes the interior of wealthy New Mexican homes:

> The houses throughout the country are furnished with mattresses, doubled up and arranged close to the walls, so as to answer for seats; these are covered with beautiful Navajo blankets, worth from 50 to 100 dollars. The walls, midway up, are covered with calico, to prevent the whitewash rubbing off; and the whole interior of the houses of the wealthy is covered with mirrors. All the hidalgos (Spanish-born) pride themselves on allowing nothing but silver to approach their tables; even the plates are of silver. But, with all this air of wealth, true comfort is wanting; and very few of our blessed land would consent to live like the wealthiest Rico in New Mexico (*Abert's New Mexico Report*, 52).

Patriotic Celebration

Before the American invasion, the Patriotic Council in Santa Fe passed a resolution on September 12, 1844, to authorize the purchase of various alcohols, cakes, cookies, and candies for an upcoming celebration. In addition to forty-three bottles of wine and twenty-five bottles of aguardiente, the menu included *marquesotes* (a spongecake made of sugar, almond, and eggs); *puches* (a doughnut-like cookie); red, blue, and gold *coronas* (crowns) cookies; *soletas* (a meringue-type cookie made with egg whites, sugar, almonds, and a little flour); *dulces* (candy) made from sugar and eggs; and *biscochos de regalo* (cookies made with flour, sugar, lard and butter).

The wine and aguardiente were combined with sugar, cinnamon, coffee, and spices to make punch, and mistela was also served. The council paid forty pesos for these refreshments ("Records of the 11th Session," Patriotic Council, Santa Fe, September 12, 1844).

Puches

Mix water with texquite and let sit for 6 minutes. Strain out solids and save the liquid to add to recipe. With beater, cream the shortening with the sugar until fluffy, adding sugar gradually. Mix dry ingredients: flour, salt, anise, and baking powder. To creamed shortening, add the eggs and dry ingredients, beating steadily. Then, beat in the rum. Refrigerate the dough for 6 hours. Flour your hands, then pinch off English walnut-sized balls of dough. Dip balls in flour and roll out between hands to make a five-inch-long rope, approximately one-half-inch in diameter. Shape into a loop or ring with overlapping ends well pressed together. Bake on an ungreased cookie sheet at 350º F. for 20 minutes, or until delicate brown. Be quick forming the loops, as the batter is soft like a cake batter. (Translated by Sam Arnold from Nuevo Cocinero Mejicano.)

*Texquite, or more correctly, tequesquite, is a crude sodium bicarbonate that forms on the banks of mineral springs in New Mexico. It is also found near several New Mexico lakes. According to Curtin, cocineras, or cooks, wanting specially light and fluffy cakes substituted tequesquite for commercial baking powder.

2 tablespoons water
2 teaspoons texquite,* a native leavening agent from New Mexico (substitute baking soda)
4-¾ cups sifted flour
1 teaspoon baking powder
1 teaspoon anise seed
1 teaspoon salt
1-½ cups shortening
1 cup sugar
4 eggs, well beaten
2 ounces dark rum

Marquesotes, or Marquis Cakes

Beat the eggs well, mixing lots of air in them. While beating, add the sugar and ground almonds. Gradually add the starch to make a dough. Pour it into greased iron or tin

8 eggs
1 pound sweet almonds, soaked overnight, then ground fine
½ pound sugar
½ pound corn starch

cookie molds and bake in a medium-hot oven. These may also be baked on a comal. They are noble cookies, well suited to a marquis's taste (Translated by Sam Arnold from Nuevo Cocinero Mejicano.)

Soletas

12 egg whites, beaten stiff
1-¾ pounds sugar
32 egg yolks, beaten

Mix ingredients, shape into cakes, and drop onto waxed paper, leaving space between cakes. Shape the cakes as you like; some people shape them into an initial or paint a name on each cake with sugar. Bake in a 325º F. oven until just golden. Sprinkle with powdered sugar and serve. (Translated by Sam Arnold from Nuevo Cocinero Mejicano.)

References

Abert, Lieutenant James W. *Through the Country of the Comanche Indians in the Fall of the Year 1845.* Edited by John Galvin. San Francisco: John Howell Books, 1970.

[Abert, Lieutenant James W.] *Abert's New Mexico Report, 1846–47.* Alburquerque: Horn and Wallace, 1962.

Curtin, L.M.S. *Healing Herbs of the Upper Rio Grande.* Los Angeles: Southwest Museum, 1965.

The Española Valley Cookbook. Española, N.M.: The Española Hospital Auxliary, 1974.

Ferguson, Erna. *Mexican Cookbook.* Albuquerque: University of New Mexico Press, 1945.

Gilbert, Mrs. Fabiola C. de Baca. *Historic Cookery.* Circular 161. State College, N. M.: Extension Service of New Mexico College of Agriculture and Mechanic Arts, 1950.

Granado, Diego. *Libro del Arte Cozina, 1599.* Owned by the Hispanic Society of America, New York, N.Y. Microfilm.

Gregg, Josiah. *Commerce of the Prairies.* Vol. 1. New York: Henry G. Langley, 1844. Reprint. Keystone Western Americana Series. Edited by Archibald Hanna and William H. Goetzmann. New York and Philadelphia: J. J. Lippincott Company, 1962.

Magoffin, Susan Shelby. *Down the Santa Fe Trail and Into Mexico: The Diary of Susan Shelby Magoffin, 1846–1847.* Edited by Stella M. Drumm. New Haven, Conn.: Yale University Press, 1926.

New Mexico. Patriotic Council, Santa Fe. *Records of the 11th Session*, September 12, 1844. New Mexico Record Center Archives.

Nuevo Cocinero Mejicano, En Forma de Diccionario. 1903 ed. Mexico City/Paris: Libreria de la Vida de Ch. Bouret, 1831.

Sahagún, Fray Bernardino de. *General History of the Things of New Spain* (Florentine Codex). Vol. 8, Kings and Lords. Part 9. Translated from the Aztec by Arthur J. D. Anderson and Charles Dibble. Santa Fe: Monographs of the School of American Research, No. 14. The School of American Research and the University of Utah, 1979.

Santa Fe Republican. 1847. New Mexico Historical Library. Microfiche.

Ward, Henry G. *Mexico in 1827.* Vol. 1. London: Colburn, 1828.

Epilogue

Au Revoir and Shinin' Times

When considering the westward movement over the Santa Fe Trail from 1821 to 1870, one should always err on the side of sophistication. While dog stew and simple, often crude dishes were generally the rule in trapper camps or military campaigns, eating had become a stylish and cosmopolitan activity in the West. In 1849, San Francisco restaurants were serving elaborate multicourse dinners with the menus all in French. Far from being the "boonies," Santa Fe in 1848 had experienced a quarter-century of trade with St. Louis and Westport, Missouri, and was supplied with goods from all over the civilized world. From New York, Philadelphia, Boston, New Orleans, London, and Paris, hard and soft goods, fine wines, champagne, and oysters all came across the Santa Fe Trail, earlier than we might have guessed.

Now, a century-and-a-half later, we're finding excitement and good eating in the food heritage of the Mexican and Native American, a heritage too long ignored by the culinarians of America. Today, top creative restaurant chefs are discovering a new world of food products such as chiles, blue corn, and native seed grains.

I hope that this book will be a stepping-stone for future food historians. Please examine the odd and the esoteric found here with an open mind and an explorer's palate. Since many of the recipes retain their nineteenth-century wording, you may want to use them more as guideposts. Remember, recipes are like roadmaps — how you travel and where you end up depends on you. Waugh!

Index

Abert, James W.: on eating skunk, 42; on kinnikinnik, 55; on pickled devil's claw, 75; on making corn-sugar molasses, 90; on grape picking at Bernalillo; on the Santa Fe market, 104; on piñon nuts, 119; on homes of wealthy New Mexicans, 121
Acorn meal, 53–54
Aguardiente, 26, 88
Alcohol: doped or diluted, 43–44; trading for, in an Indian encampment, 45; trade, and Bent's Fort, 78–79. *See also* Whiskey
Allegheny Whiskey, 23
Almond Atole, 85
American Fur Company, 44
Antelope, tolling (hunting method) for, 41
Apple Pie Without Apples, or Mock Apple Pie, 63
Applejack, 31
Arbuckle Brothers, 21
Army Bread, 62–63
Arrow Rock (Mo.), 1–3
Arroz Dulce, 115
Atole and chaquehue, 85–86
    Recipe: **Almond Atole, 85**
Aubry, Francis X., 105
Austin, Stephen F., 11

Bacon. *See* Salt pork
Baird, James, 88
Barclay, Alexander, 72–74
Basic Red Chile Puree, 111
Bearberry leaves, preparing for smoking, 56
Beaver tail, preparing, 80–81
Becknell, William, 1
Beef: **Roasting Beef, 7–8**
Bent, Charles, 71, 88, 104. *See also* Bent's Fort
Bent, William (bro. of Charles), 5, 71. *See also* Bent's Fort
Bent, St. Vrain & Company, 63. *See also* Bent's Fort; St. Vrain & Bent Company
Benton, Thomas Hart, 59
Bent's Fort, 26; building of, and daily life in, 71–72; food stuffs at, 72–

76; good times at, 76; wine and luxury goods at, 77–78; liquor trade and, 78–79; drinks at, 79–80, 83; beaver tail at, and how to prepare, 80–81
    Recipes: **Hailstorm, 79**
        Molasses Taffy, 78
        Pickled Devil's Claws, 75–76
        Pumpkin Pie, 74
        Slap Jacks, 75
        Wassail, 80
Bent's Water Biscuits, 74
Beverages. *See* Applejack; Chocolate; Cocktails; Coffee; Eggnog; **Hailstorm; Licor de Yerba Buena;** Mexican cold drinks (refrescos); **Mistela;** Rum; Shrubs; **Spruce Beer;** Teas; **Wassail;** Whiskey; Wine
Biscochitos, 96
Bitters. *See* Cocktails
Booz, E. C., 25
Boston Corn Bread, 12
Bottles: for whiskey, 25–26; for wine, 77
Boudins, 39; Garrard on, 34
Bourbon, 23–24
Bread, in the New Mexican marketplace, 104. *See also* **Army Bread;** *Corn breads; Fried breads;* Piki; Sourdough
Bread pudding. *See* **Capirotada, or Spotted Dog**
Brewerton, George, 27
Broiled Mackerel, 66
Budin de Garbanzo, 119
Buffalo: hunting and eating, on the Santa Fe Trail, 33–35; Mexican hunters of, 35–37; jerky, 37–38; tongue, 39–40. *See also* Boudins; *Jerked meat*
    Recipes: **Buffalo en Appolas, 35**
        Buffalo Tongue, 40
        Carne seca, or jerky, to prepare, 38
        Marrow bones, to broil, 38
Burnham, Jesse, 10
Byrd, John, 23

Cajeta de Leche, 116
Cakes: **Marquesotes, or Marquis Cakes, 122–23**
        Puches, 122
        Soletas, 123
Caldo de Cordero, 120
Camino Real, 4, 91
Camp Fire Coffee, 22
Capirotada, or Spotted Dog, 118
Carleton, J. Henry, 46
Carne Adobada, 113
Carne seca, 37–38; preparing, 38. *See also Jerked meat*
Catfish: **To Fry Catfish, 4–5**
Catfish House, 4
Champurrado, 87
Chapman, Arthur, 18
Chaquehue. *See* Atole and chaquehue
Cheese: **New Mexico Goat's Milk Cheese, 117**
        Requesones, 117
Chia seed, 85
Chicken: **Pollo Relleno, 100**
        Shaker Chicken Fricassee, 7
        Stewed Hen in Red Chile, 99
Chile con Carne, 113
Chiles, 109–15
    Recipes: **Basic Red Chile Puree, 111**
        Carne Adobada, 113
        Chile con Carne, 113
Chimajá Whiskey, 95
Chipita (gen'l. housekeeper at Bent's Fort), 78, 86
Chocolate, in Mexico, 103
    Recipes: **Champurrado, 87**
        Hot Chocolate, 22
        Mexican Chocolate, 102
        Mexican Chocolate, Short Version, 102
Chokecherries, 49; tea from bark of, 22, 55; in pemmican, 48
    Recipe: **Wo-ja-pi, 50**
Ciboleros, 35–37
Cimarron cutoff, 71
Cocktails, 26–28
    Recipes: **Hot Brandy and Rum Punch, 28**

Cocktail Recipes continued
> Martinez Gin Cocktail, 27
> The Real Georgia Mint Julep, 28
> Sazerac, 27
Coffee, 21–22; in army rations, 64
> *Recipes:* Camp Fire Coffee, 22
> Mexican Pot Coffee, 87
Coffin, Morse H., 80
Colcannon, 69
Colonche and lemonade with chia, 84–85
Commote, 52–53
Cookies. *See* Desserts
Coon, Benjamin F., 105
Corn, in Texas, 10, 14–15. *See also* Hominy
> *Recipes:* Corn and Bean Soup, 101
> Green Corn Fritters, 11
Corn and Bean Soup, 101
Corn Breads (*see also* Cornmeal):
> Boston Corn Bread, 12
> Corn Bread (St. Charles Hotel), 12
> Indian Loaf Cake, 13
> Johnnie Cake, 13
> New England Corn Cake, 11
> Southern Cornmeal Pone, or Corn Dodgers, 14
> Spider Corn Cake, 14
> Virginia Corn Bread, 12
Corn dodgers. *See* Southern Cornmeal Pone, or Corn Dodgers
Cornmeal, as a staple, 10–11, 14, 53. *See also* Atole and chaquehue; *Corn breads*; Hominy; Pinole and champurrado
> *Recipes:* Indian Meal Pudding, 67
> Slap Jacks, 75
> Was-nah, 51

Desserts (*see also Cakes; Pies*):
> Arroz Dulce, 115
> Bischochitos
> Budin de Garbanzo, 119
> Cajeta de Leche, 116
> Capirotada, or Spotted Dog, 118
> Eagle Brand Cajeta, 116–17
> New Mexico Goat's Milk Cheese, 117
> Requesones, 117
> Sopaipillas Made with Baking Powder, 98
> Sopaipillas Made with Yeast, 97
Devil's claws. *See* Pickled Devil's Claws
Dodge, Henry, 45
Dog stew, 45–48

Doughnuts. *See Fried breads*
Dutch oven, 17–18

Eagle Brand Cajeta, 116–17
Eggs: Machaca de Huevo, 93
Eggnog, 88–89
> *Recipes:* Old-Time Eggnog, 89
> Taos Hanging Eggnog, 89
Estis's Tavern (Taos, N.M.), 88

Finker, 68
Fish: Broiled Mackerel, 66
> To Fry Catfish, 4–5
Fitzpatrick, Thomas, 37
Foodstuffs: on the Santa Fe Trail, 4; at Bent's Fort, 72–74; advertised in Santa Fe, 104–5
Forts: along the Santa Fe Trail, 59–60; mealtime at, 60–62; wild game and, 63; staple diet in, 63–67
> *Recipes:* Apple Pie Without Apples, or Mock Apple Pie, 63
> Army Bread, 62–63
> Broiled Mackerel, 66
> Colcannon, 69
> Finker, 68
> Hardcrackers, or Hard Tack, 62
> Indian Meal Pudding, 67
> Plain Irish Stew for Fifty Men, 65
> St. Jacob's Soup, 68
> Salt Pork with Mashed Peas for One Hundred Men, 64
> Spruce Beer, 67
> Stewed Oysters, 66
> Suet Dumplings, 65
> Turkish Pilaf for One Hundred Men, 65–66
Four-Seed Horchata, 84
Fowl, wild, 42
Fremont, John C., 45
Fried breads: Olykoeks (Oily Cakes, or Raised Doughnuts), 19
> Squaw Bread, 53

Gall, 54–55
Garbanzos, 101
> *Recipes:* Budin de Garbanzo, 119
> Garbanzos with Chile, 101–2
Garrard, Lewis, 41, 49, 83; on buffalo, 33–35; on dog stew, 46–48; on an evening at Bent's Fort, 76
Glass bottles: for whiskey, 25–26; for wine, 77

Goat's milk. *See* Cajeta de Leche; New Mexico Goat's Milk Cheese; Requesones
Granado, Diego, 118
Green, Dick, 72, 74
Green, Charlotte (wife of Dick), 72, 74, 76
Gregg, Josiah, 88, 106; on cibolero's camp, 36–37; on piñon nuts, 119
Grinnell, George Bird: on a wagon train mess, 5–6; on liquor trading in an Indian village, 45; on Independence Day at Bent's Fort, 79
Guayave. *See* Piki

Hailstorm, 79
Hardcrackers, or Hard Tack, 62
Harris, John, 4
Harris House Hotel (Westport, Mo.), 4
Hays House (Council Grove, Kans.), 7
Herbal teas, 22
Hess, Dexter, 76
Hominy, 107–9; how to make, 15–16. *See also* Posole; Tamales; Tortillas
> *Recipe:* Champurrado, 87
Honey, 98
Horchata, 83
Hot Brandy and Rum Punch, 28
Hot Chocolate, 22
Houston, Sam, 15
La Houton (Baron), 2
Hudson's Bay Company, 24
Hunting methods: for buffalo, 33–37; for antelope, 41

Indian groups: relations of, among themselves and with whites, 43, 59; alcohol trade with, 43–45; foods of, on the Plains, 45–49, 52–58; cooking and eating among, 49–50, 56–58
> *Recipes:* Squaw Bread, 53
> Wash-tunk-ala, 52
> Was-nah, 51
> Wo-ja-pi, 50
Indian Loaf Cake, 13
Indian Meal Pudding, 67
Injun Whiskey, 25
Innards, 54–55
> *Recipe:* Finker, 68
Irving, John Treat, Jr., 56–57

Jerked meat: Wash-tunk-ala, 52
Johnnie Cake, 13

Kearney, Stephen W., 64; invasion path of, 90–91
Kinnikinnik, 55–56

Lamb (see also *Mutton*): **Caldo de Cordero,** 120
Lemonade. *See* Colonche and lemonade with chia
Licor de Yerba Buena, 95
Loves Horses, 51

McGee, Allen, 4
McGee Tavern and Hotel (Westport, Mo.), 4
Machaca de Huevo, 93
Magoffin, Samuel, 99, 109
Magoffin, Susan (wife of Samuel), 8, 26, 31, 100, 104; on eating grulla (sand cranes), 42; on trading glass bottles, 77; on Mexican cooking, 99; on chocolate, 102; on chiles, 109–10
Mahaffie House (near Westport, Mo.), 6
Marquesotes, or Marquis Cakes, 122–23
Marrow bones, to broil, 38
Martinez Gin Cocktail, 27
Masa. *See* Cornmeal
Masa Harina. *See* Hominy
Mexican Chocolate, 102
Mexican Chocolate, Short Version, 102
Mexican cold drinks (refrescoes), 83–85
    Recipes: Four-Seed Horchata, 84
            Horchata, 83
Mexican Pot Coffee, 87
Mistela, 94–95
Molasses, long sweet and corn-sugar, 90
    Recipe: Molasses Taffy, 78
Monongahela Whiskey, 23
Moose Nose, 40–41
Morino, Antonio, 110
Mormons, 68
Mortar and pestle, 56
Mountain Branch, 71
Mutton (see also *Lamb*): **Plain Irish Stew for Fifty Men,** 65

Nave, Henry, 2
New England Corn Cake, 11
New Mexico: foods and drinks in, 93–103, 105–23; market in, 103–4; sheep ranching in, 120; Abert's report of breakfast and homes of wealthy in, 121
    Recipes: Arroz Dulce, 115
            Basic Red Chile Puree, 111
            Biscochitos, 96
            Budin de Garbanzo, 119

Cajeta de Leche, 116
Caldo de Cordero, 120
Capirotada, or Spotted Dog, 118
Carne Adobada, 113
Chile con Carne, 113
Chimaja Whiskey, 95
Corn and Bean Soup, 101
Eagle Brand Cajeta, 116–17
Garbanzos with Chile, 101–2
Licor de Yerba Buena, 95
Machaca de Huevo, 93
Marquesotes, or Marquis Cakes, 122–23
Mexican Chocolate, 102
Mexican Chocolate, Short Version, 102
Mistela, 94–95
New Mexico Goat's Milk Cheese, 117
Pollo Relleno, 100
Posole (Hog and Hominy), 108
Posole with Pork and Green Chile, 108–9
Puches, 122
Recipe for Tamales, 107
Requesones, 117
Soletas, 123
Sopa de Arroz, 100
Sopa de vermicelli, to prepare, 94
Sopaipillas Made with Baking Powder, 98
Sopaipillas Made with Yeast, 97
Stewed Hen in Red Chile, 99
Trotter Posole, 109
New Mexico Goat's Milk Cheese, 117
Nixtamal. *See* Hominy
Northwest Company, 24

Old-Time Eggnog, 89
Olmsted, Frederick Law, 11
Olykoeks (Oily Cakes, or Raised Doughnuts), 19
Owl Woman (wife of Wm. Bent), 72
Oysters, shipping methods for, 8
    Recipe: Stewed Oysters, 66

Parker, A. A., 11, 14
Paul, Prince of Wurttemburg, 57
Paunch cooking, 49–50

Pemmican, 48
Perry, Charles, 118
Pickled Devil's Claws, 75–76
Pies: Apple Pie Without Apples, or Mock Apple Pie, 63
        Pumpkin Pie, 74
        Rhubarb Stalks Pie, or Persian Apple, 2
Pike, Zebulon, 1
Piki, 105–6
Pinole and champurrado, 86–87
    Recipe: Champurrado, 87
Piñon nuts, 54, 119–20
Pipsissewa tea, 22
Plain Irish Stew for Fifty Men, 65
Pois de Trappeur, 10
Pollo Relleno, 100
Pomme blanche, 52
Pork, in Arrow Rock, Mo., 2. *See also* Posole; Salt pork
    Recipes: Carne Adobada, 113
            Chile con Carne, 113
Posole, 107–9
    Recipes: Posole (Hog and Hominy), 108
            Posole with Pork and Green Chile, 108–9
            Trotter Posole, 109
Prairie potatoes, 52
Puches, 122
Pumpkin Pie, 74

Rainey, T. C., 3
Raspberry Shrub, 31
The Real Georgia Mint Julep, 28
Refrescoes. *See* Colanche and lemonade with chia; Four-Seed Horchata; Horchata
Requesones, 117
Rhubarb Stalks Pie, or Persian Apple, 2
Rice: Arroz Dulce, 115
        Sopa de Arroz, 100
        Turkish Pilaf for One Hundred Men, 65–66
Richard brothers, 88
Rickey, Don, 61
Riley, Bennett, 60
Roasting Beef, 7–8
Roberts, Benjamin Morgan, 68
Rocky Mountain Punch, 30
Rum, 28–30; in army rations, 64
    Recipes: Hot Brandy and Rum Punch, 28
            Rocky Mountain Punch, 30
            Rum Shrub, 32
            Tom & Jerry, 30
Ruxton, George Frederick, 74

Sage, Rufus B., 84; on alcohol trade with Indians, 44; on Christmas Day, 1841, meal with was-nah, 51; on virtues of buffalo gall, 54–55
St. Jacob's Soup, 68
St. Vrain, Ceran, 33, 71, 100. *See also* Bent's Fort
St. Vrain, Marcellus (bro. of Ceran), 41
St. Vrain & Bent Company, 104. *See also* Bent, St. Vrain & Company
Salt: processing of, at Boone's Lick, 3; lack of, in Indian foods, 46, 52
Salt pork: as a staple meat, 8–9; in army rations, 61, 64
    Recipes: **Recipe for Salt Pork, 9**
        Salt Pork with Mashed Peas for One Hundred Men, 64
        St. Jacob's Soup, 68
San Jacinto corn, 14–15
Santa Anna, Antonio López de, 15
Santa Fe (city) Patriotic Council, 121–22
Santa Fe Trail: early history of, 1; wagon train assembling for, 3; freighting on, 4; meals on, 5–6. *See also* Bent's Fort; Cimarron cutoff
Sappington, John, 2
Sazerac, 27
Shaker Chicken Fricassee, 7
Shaker settlements, 6
Sherman, William Tecumseh, 60
Shrubs, 31–32
    Recipes: **Raspberry Shrub, 31**
        Rum Shrub, 32
Skunk, 42
Slap Jacks, 75
Smith, Peg-leg, 88
Smith, Uncle John, 46
Smithwick, Noah, 10
Smoking mixtures. *See* Kinnikinnik
Soletas, 123
Sopa de Arroz, 100
Sopa de vermicelli, to prepare, 94
Sopaipillas Made with Baking Powder, 98
Sopaipillas Made with Yeast, 97
Soups: **Corn and Bean Soup, 101**
        Pois de Trappeur, 10
        Sopa de Arroz, 100
        Sopa de vermicelli, to prepare, 94
Sourdough, 16–18; biscuits in a Dutch oven, 17–18
    Recipe: **Sourdough Starter and Bread, 16–17**
Southern Cornmeal Pone, or Corn Dodgers, 14
Spider Corn Cake, 14
Split peas. *See* **Pois de Trappeur**

Spotted Dog. *See* **Capirotada, or Spotted Dog**
Spruce Beer, 67–68
Squaw Bread, 53
Stewed Hen in Red Chile, 99
Stewed Oysters, 66
Suet Dumplings, 65
Sumac berries, 55. *See also* **Wo-ja-pi**

Tamales, 106–7
    Recipe: **Recipe for Tamales, 107**
Taos Hanging Eggnog, 89
Taos Lightning, 26, 87–88
Teas, 22
Thomas, Jerry, 27, 30
Tom & Jerry, 30
Tongue, See Buffalo
Tortillas, 105
Trotter Posole, 109
Turkish Pilaf for One Hundred Men, 65–66

United States Hotel (Santa Fe, N.M.), 27

Vial, Pedro, 1
Virginia Corn Bread, 12

Wash-tunk-ala, 52
Was-nah, 51
Wassail, 80
Webster, A. L. (Mrs.), 22–23
Whiskey: importation into, and distilling of, in the West, 23–26, 87–88. *See also* Indian groups
    Recipes: **Chimaja Whiskey, 95**
        Injun Whiskey, 25
Wine: at Bent's Fort, 77; production of, in El Paso, 91–92
Wittenmeyer, Annie, 66
Wo-ja-pi, 50
Workman, William, 23